Puffy & Blue

THE CHRONICLES OF NINE LIVES TOGETHER

Puffy & Blue, The Chronicles of Nine Lives Together
by Kayla Fioravanti

Editor-in-Chief: Loral Robben Pepoon
Editing & Critique Team: Debbie Richards, Robin Schmidt, Rose Cunfer and Nora Kilbourne

Cover Art: Lisa Rodgers of Shoot Y'all Photography
Cover Design: Jennifer Smith

ISBN-13: 978-0692381274 (Selah Press)
ISBN-10: 0692381279

Printed in the United States of America
Published by Selah Press

Notice of Rights: All rights reserved. No part of this book may be reproduced or transmitted in any form by any means, electronic, mechanical, photocopy, recording or other without the prior written permission of the publisher.

Disclaimer: The author and publisher have left out names and identifying details to protect the privacy of individuals. The author has tried to recreate events, locales and conversations from the author's memory of them. In order to maintain privacy the author and publisher have in some instances left out the name and identifying details of individuals. Although the author and publisher have made every effort to make sure all information is correct at press time, the author and publisher do not assume and hereby disclaim any liability to any party for any loss, damage, disruptions caused by stories with this book, whether such information is a result of errors or emission, accident, slander or other cause.

For information on getting permission for reprints and excerpts, contact: info@Selah-Press.com

Author Website: KaylaFioravanti.com

Photographer Website: Shootyallphotography.com

Copyright © 2014 Kayla Fioravanti

Dedication

I am thankful for all the cats who have given me comfort, unconditional love and companionship. I have been blessed by the lives of Puffy, Smokey, Sweet William, Zen, Ena, Puffin, Seamus, Casey, Gibby, Star, Gogo, Boo, Riley, Sadie and Yeti over the span of my life. My mom, brother and I shared a great love for cats growing up. That love has spread to my children Keegan, Selah and Caiden. This one goes to the cats. Of all God's creations great and small, the cat ranks among my favorite.

Contents

Foreword

1	Before Puffy & Blue (1963-1967)	1
2	Dallas, Texas (1967-1968)	5
3	Tachikawa, Japan (1968-1972)	9
4	San Mateo, California (1972)	17
5	Desoto, Texas (1972-1976)	29
6	Munich, Germany (1976-1981)	49
7	Duncanville, Texas (1981-1984)	89
8	San Antonio Texas (1984-1986)	103
9	Portland, Oregon (1986-1992)	125
10	After Puffy (1992)	145

Foreword

Family, faith and pets. These were three of the constants in our lives as our father's job with the Army and Air Force Exchange Service (AAFES) took us from house to house, town to town, state to state and country to country. Every time we picked up to move to a new assignment, we left behind friends and started the process again of finding new ones.

With each move, another set of challenges faced us, whether it was a bully that wanted to intimidate the new kid or a health crisis that threatened the life of a loved one. But, no matter the challenge or location, we were together as a family. Each of us had our strengths and our weaknesses, but our bonds withstood all the tests put in front of us.

At the center of our family was faith. We were raised with strong Christian values and they helped guide us through our formative years. As young adults, the strength of our faith weakened somewhat and that threw off our moral compass. But that Christian faith was implanted deep in us so that it could blossom once again as we matured.

As for the third constant, I'm not really sure if "pet" is the accurate label, because the animals in our lives were more like members of the family. From our earliest memories, we've had an animal companion in our household. Even as Kayla and I grew into adults and formed our own families, we included animals in our lives. I think the importance of pets goes back to our nomadic upbringing. Through the heartache and chaos of moving, we had a core group of furry friends who would be our playmates and our soul mates. They could somehow sense when we were down and needed that extra bit of attention.

For Kayla, that companion was her cat Puffy. It's this healing relationship that is at the heart of this book. I was aware of some of the struggles that Kayla faced growing up, but not to the extent of what she reveals in this book. It pains me to discover the depth of her sorrows, but it comforts me to know that she came out the other side as a strong, creative and loving human being.

The way Kayla grew up is probably very different than the way you did, but as you read her story, I'm sure that you'll find moments that seem familiar. By reading about her hardships and the way she ultimately overcame them, you'll find inspiration for your own trials and tribulations.

I am proud of my sister and I am so glad that she had a friend like Puffy to be with her through everything. We all should be lucky enough to have a Puffy in our lives.

Kevin Mohs, (Kayla's Big Brother), author of *The Devil's Bite*

Chapter 1
Before Puffy & Blue (1963–1967)

You may wonder, *"Who is Puffy? Who is Blue?"* I was given the nickname Blue in 1985, when I took on the habit of wearing bright blue boots, blue eyeliner, blue eye shadow and blue mascara. The bright blue boots were in rebellion to becoming an unwilling resident of San Antonio, Texas. To show my stark contrast to the typical brown, black or gray leather cowboy boots that Texans wore, I wore bright blue suede boots. I adorned my eyes with bright blue eye shadow, eyeliner and mascara because it was the 1980's, I was a girl and I lived in Texas. Each of these reasons qualify as good excuse—I am clinging to all three of them.

As a teenager, I worked at Albertson's Grocery store, where I had to wear a uniform. I always accented my uniform with my blue boots. I loved outwardly being a nonconformist, especially in my work uniform. During those years I did everything to blatantly and subtly not assimilate to the world around me. My whole life I had also resisted nicknames. I loved my name—Kayla—why trade it for something less? But in San Antonio, the nickname "Blue" fit me. Not only did I wear blue on the outside, but also I was deeply blue and sad on the inside.

My cat Puffy was given her name when we adopted her. She looked like a puff of smoke. At home we already had a black cat named Smokey. Puffy looked like a tiny puff of smoke next to Smokey. This book contains stories from my life during Puffy's twenty-one year life span. The book is about me, my family, our travels and our pets. It is about Puffy and the lessons she taught me along the way. Puffy defined and hemmed in my childhood. She was part of my family before I ever went to pre-school, and she was there just before I graduated from college.

Puffy and I travelled the world together. We encountered tarantulas, armadillos, hedge hogs, lizards, scorpions, field mice, squirrels, birds, rabbits and more. We had two other pets that lived with Puffy and me. Puffy took care of the other pets just as much as I did—sometimes even more. Puffy was an adventuresome cat. Our lives were lived out on three different continents. Puffy's native language was Japanese, but she quickly learned my native language, English. I am convinced, however, that she never learned to speak German when we moved there. Together Puffy and I lived in Tachikawa, Japan; San Mateo, California; Desoto, Texas; Munich, Germany; Duncanville, Texas; San Antonio, Texas; Nieder Roden, Germany and finally Portland, Oregon. My entire childhood was encapsulated by the years of her life.

As a kid it was hard to imagine that my family had a life before I arrived, but I guess they did. I've heard stories and seen the black and white photographs to prove it. Their lives were full of joy, struggle, adventure and pets. Before Puffy and me, there was my brother Kevin, a pregnancy that ended in miscarriage, a rambunctious Dalmatian named Bitsy, a Siamese cat named Casey and my parents. Even during my mom's pregnancy with me, there was an ongoing family story. I was part of that story, but unaware of it until much later.

My parents' lives together started in college. My dad had just gotten a box of chocolate chip cookies in the mail from his mom when he spotted my mom. He bragged that he had made the cookies as he offered her one and asked her out. I guess she was either impressed with his culinary skills or by his handsome looks, because they went out. On their very first date my dad knew—and told my mom—that he was going to marry her.

Even when my parents were dating, cats were in their lives. The cat whose story impressed me the most was named Dubby. He liked to go swimming with my parents. I have seen the photographs of this feat, so I know that the tale is true. But knowing how terrified my mother and most cats are of water makes the story remarkable.

My parents got married during Christmas break of their senior year at Mankato State in Minnesota. Shortly after graduation, they took off to see the world. They were both from small towns. My dad was a farm boy from Medford, Minnesota, with big dreams of traveling. My mom was from Bismarck, North Dakota. She had a creative artistic streak that helped her absorb the world and reflect it back to us even more beautifully in her art. My dad was recruited to work for AAFES (Army Air Force Exchange Service) with promises of being stationed worldwide. Their first station was in Lawton, Oklahoma.

They drove an old beat up Volkswagen Bug across the country to their new home. It wasn't Paris, but it wasn't where they had been either. It was the beginning of many transfers. My brother Kevin was born in Lawton, Oklahoma. And shortly after Oklahoma they would be transferred to San Antonio, Texas and then Dallas, Texas, where I was born.

Chapter 2
Dallas, Texas (1967–1968)

In Dallas, Texas, my parents got the shock of their lives. While my mom was pregnant with me, she was diagnosed with Hodgkin's disease. The news continued to reverberate in our lives for decades. My mom put my life above her own and refused all treatment during pregnancy. She wouldn't even allow the surgeons to sedate her for the biopsy. She wanted no harm to come to me in any effort to extend her life. As I grew, so did the cancer, but she actually lost weight during pregnancy as her body suffered the consequences of the disease.

My mom always told me that I was a most wanted child. In my mom's words:

> *Finally the special night came. I had one false alarm a few days before, but on this day September 18, 1967, there was no false alarm. You were about to present yourself to the world.*
>
> *Your Dad and I, along with Kevin, had been waiting for you for a long time. Yes, Kevin too. He loved to put his hand on my stomach and feel you move inside of me. We took Kevin to our friends, the Clocks, while your dad rushed me to the hospital. There was no need to rush, but your dad was most anxious for us to be in the safe hands of others.*
>
> *We checked into the hospital around six o'clock in the evening. The doctor was a woman by the name of Dr. Finely. She was an attractive fashionable woman. She had a very nice neat figure, dark hair, which she wore up, and she had carefully applied make-up. Your dad and Dr. Finely enjoyed a conversation as they stood around the labor table.*
>
> *I had been given a shot that would hurry you into the world. You needed little help, because you were most eager to be born. So eager that I had to tell your dad and the doctor that you were pushing your way out of me. They*

ignored me and continued talking. I pushed extra hard. The doctor had just scolded me for eating chili before coming to the hospital.

After that I yelled, "The baby is coming!"

The doctor lifted the sheet and saw your head.

The doctor yelled, "Oh my God!"

She called for nurses and a table with wheels. They quickly put me on that table and wheeled me down the corridor toward the delivery room. You were coming so fast that they put the gas mask on my face so I would sleep and the delivery would slow down. I regretted this because we had planned that I would not be given anything, so I could watch you be born into this world. I had looked so forward to this moment.

Everything was happening so fast. I was out for a very short time.

I woke up to the doctor flopping you on top of my stomach and saying, "Here is your little girl!"

I quickly dozed off. The next time I saw you, you were all cleaned and wrapped up. They took me to my room with a promise that during the night they would bring you to me. It was now only a short time after ten o'clock. They kept their promise and early the next morning, just at sunrise, they brought you in. We were left completely alone. You had just been fed your first food.

I had all the time I needed to look you over. I checked your fingers, toes, legs, arms—every part of you. You looked perfect. I wish I had the words to express to you, Kayla, describing how a mom feels when she looks at her baby, especially her girl baby. It was one of my closest moments to God. The birth of your brother was another one of those moments.

I felt there was a light in me—a joy with no bounds—I had given life to another human being. God used me as an instrument to carry one of his children. An act of love, between your dad and me, had given birth to a beautiful baby girl.

Your dad, Kevin and I were living in Dallas surrounded by friends. These friends were needed at this time. I was ill and you needed care. Friends took care of you while I was in the hospital. A woman by the name of Jean took you, a two-week-old baby, into her home while I went back into the hospital. As I was being treated, you were being loved and cared for.

After a time, I was able to care for you. You were such a good baby. It was almost like you knew I was sick. You cried very little and smiled a great deal. How fortunate we were!

Your brother loved you immediately. He was happy to have you in our family and always wanted to hold you.

I couldn't hold you because of my left arm—but your dad and brother made up for it. I put your infant chair up on top of your walker and then I could easily move you about from room to room. I talked to you all the time. You listened carefully and would eagerly reply. Since I couldn't carry you, I kept you with me. We also spent a lot of time in the rocking chair. We had a good time together."

As soon as I was born, my mom started treatment. Friends and family came to our aid. At the time Hodgkin's disease was a death sentence, and my mom's delayed treatment didn't help her prognosis.

I know I was there for those early years, but I don't remember them. As a child, I actually thought that when I was in the womb, I was fighting a long battle of *Cowboys and Indians*. In those days, playing *Cowboys and Indians* was politically correct. I watched Lone Ranger and Tonto, and was huge fan. In my memories, I spent a great deal of time hunkered down behind a large boulder. Later, when my mom taught me the facts of life, I was in great disbelief about what really happened in the womb. But then again, maybe I was fighting a battle in the womb in my own way. Maybe my mom was the boulder; maybe I hid behind it, and cancer was the enemy. In the context of my memory, playing *Cowboys and Indians* was a fight for my life.

My mom's friends were always interwoven members of our family. Perhaps it was because my mom was extremely social, but I think she was always preparing us to have surrogate mom figures in our life in case she lost her battle. For a period of time, her cousin Colleen came to live with us to help my mom as she battled cancer. At other times, friends filled in and helped carry us through the years. But no matter who was helping us, my mom was always the central figure who seamlessly wove our lives together. It was as if a village raising a family was normal.

Although her cancer went into remission, my mom's illness was part of our lives for decades. She never gave up until the very end when there was nothing she could do but die with dignity and grace at her appointed time. She died much later in my life story.

For many years Dallas, Texas, was just the place I was born. I was six months old when my parents packed up their world to accept their very first transfer overseas to Tachikawa, Japan. But all military brats, and their distantly related Department of Defense brats, need an answer to give about where they are from. So, for much of my life, my answer to where I was from became Dallas, Texas. Department of Defense brats are homeless in an unusual sense, because our home is more related to the next transfer papers than a place that we will set down deep roots. We were vagabonds with no roots and no hometown. We lived an organized gypsy childhood.

Chapter 3
Tachikawa, Japan (1968–1972)

Cats in Japan

My very first memory in life is very much without context. I was about two-and-a-half years old at the time. I was standing beside the railroad tracks in Tachikawa, Japan, with my parents calling, "Casey, here kitty, kitty, kitty," in what I am certain was the sweetest little voice ever.

We were searching for our lost cat. I have absolutely no memory of Casey, yet my hazy early memory starts there beside the railroad tracks. I remember that the burnt smell of the tracks tickled my nose. I was trying to balance my wee little feet on loose gravel and stones. The scene feels black and white to me, like an old photograph. I imagine that maybe I was wearing my Mary Jane shoes and a pink jacket with a fuzzy lining. My favorite color in Japan was pink.

We never found Casey. I know from old pictures that Casey was a Siamese cat. From the stories my parents used to tell, I know Casey loved to hide and jump out to scare my dad. Once my dad jumped and screamed, Casey would prance away, satisfied. But that is all I know about Casey.

My brother also had a cat named Smokey in Texas. The story I heard is that my parents had been unable to afford to bring Smokey with them to Japan. They promised my then three-and-a-half-year-old brother that they would get him a new kitten when they got to Japan.

Their plane no sooner touched down in Japan and my brother was asking, "Where's Smokey?"

Despite their best efforts, Kevin was determined to have Smokey there with him in Japan, so when they got him a new kitten, they also named him Smokey. Smokey was never Smokey the Second or Smokey Junior. He was simply Smokey.

What I remember clearly about losing Casey, as if it were yesterday, is when we went to go get a new cat to replace Casey, I got to choose and claim the next cat. I was very excited. We went to someone's home to meet a litter of kittens.

I burst through the doorway full of colorful energy, smelling of dirt and maple syrup. Black little kittens were everywhere. The one that caught my eye instantly dashed to safety when she was startled by my commotion. The sudden motion attracted me. I fell instantly and hopelessly in love with the only kitten hiding from me.

"I want this one!" I declared as I dropped to my knees peering behind the couch.

My mom pleaded with me to view the other kittens. She pointed out that all the other kittens didn't hide. She encouraged me to pick one of them. I refused and waited patiently for the owner of the kittens to fetch the small black puff of fuzzy fur from behind the couch. We named her Puffy, because she looked like a small puff of our other cat, Smokey.

From that day forward Puffy had the difficult task of raising me. I wasn't much of a listener so Puffy had to teach by example. Sometimes the lessons were hard on both of us, as we each believed that we were raising the other. I loved Puffy, and she understood me.

Growing up, all of my best friends lived within the walls of my home. My circle included my brother, mom, dad and our pets. Because we moved every few years, it was handy for me to keep my circle within the confines of my family.

Puffy was in all ways my cat. I had chosen her and she had chosen me. We did everything together. She faithfully followed me all over the house, neighborhood and to school. She went out regularly into the world to find prizes that she would proudly deposit at my feet. She slept with me, and when I cried, she licked away the tears. I loved her dearly.

Other Faithful Friends in Japan

In the early years in Japan, we had a maid. My mom would beg her to refrain from spoiling me, but she loved me something fierce. I didn't speak Japanese and she barely spoke a word of English, but she spoke volumes through her actions. She babied me, pampered me, made me presents and even went so far as to peel every bit of the white rind from oranges before feeding them to me. I was the little blonde cherub in her care, and she simply was unable to resist the urge to spoil me with her every action.

My parents made friends in Japan who impacted our lives far into the future. My mom frolicked through Tokyo with her friends Pat and Joyce. Their friendships lasted through all of our moves. Pat's family later settled in Portland, Oregon, and Joyce's family moved back to Montana. Both of their husbands were doctors serving in the military. When their years of service were over, they opened private practices in America. Pat's husband was so moved by my mom's battle with cancer that he decided to specialize in oncology. I don't know which of our three families moved back to the States first. When we lived in America, our three families met every other summer and continued to strengthen a life-long bond of friendship.

Magical Memories

One vivid memory of my early childhood is that my mom never let me use coloring books. She didn't want me to learn to color within the lines. She taught me to use the entire piece of paper when I colored. She explained that the sky should take up at least half of the page and not be a tiny blue line at the top of the page. She encouraged me to use all the colors in the Crayola box and that people could not be expressed with only one pale color.

My mom reflected what she taught me in her own life. She greeted every stranger as an invited guest into her life. She used the entire canvas for her art and never drew inside the lines. As a child, I got messy, I dressed myself in mismatched clothes and my mom loved me unconditionally.

My dad dropped his world outside our doorway. He entered our home ready to tell stories, play games, climb mountains and engage completely. I hid in closets and around doorways ready to jump out to surprise him. He would jump—leap in fact, into the air—as he acted surprised again. He taught us the rules, life values and how to be a good citizen. He carried me to bed every night, tucked me in and kissed Puffy goodnight even though he didn't like cats. He did it because he loved people who loved cats.

My dad reflected what he taught. He lived upright, righteously and fairly in the world. He lived for, with and among our little family, as if the world revolved around the four of us.

My childhood in Japan was magical. I watched the streets turn into a fire of color and dance, as dragon heads bobbed through the crowds of song. I never knew what the people were singing, but I always sang along.

Japanese hands touched my blonde head, stroking my strands in disbelief, cooing as they petted at me. The people bought me gifts in the stores where they met me, and followed me down streets and through alleyways.

I posed for photographs with families I never knew, standing among crowds of strangers. I would wait for flash bulbs to pop, because that was the signal of my release. Today I'm sure there are pictures of a tiny blonde girl in family photo albums across the city of Tokyo.

I was an American girl wandering the streets of Tokyo with my red-haired mom. At the time I had no image to associate with the country of America. Our American Air Force base and Japan was all I had ever known. I was from behind the gates guarded by armed men in green, and that was America to me.

The hallways of the base hospital were littered with pale faced men; their frowns were so deep they never broke at the sound of my laughter. Some men had no arms and no legs; others wore so much plaster I didn't know what was left. These men had come here from Vietnam, but somehow they were all Americans, too.

When my mom and I would dance through the streets of Tokyo, I would never notice the jets piercing the air above. My mom also often rode her bike around base with me on the back of it.

When I was four years old, I was fascinated with the sounds, "*th, th, thth, th, th, thth,*" which is what I heard as the tip of my shoe toe nipped the spokes of my mom's bicycle. I loved the feeling of the wind in my hair and the warmth of the sun on my back. I was particularly fascinated with the vibrational sound that my shoe made as it flirted with the spinning spokes of the back wheel. It was the early 1970s, long before the safety gear of today's childhood was in place.

I remember it was a perfectly normal day I rode around on the back of my mom's bicycle. Again and again, I would listen to the *"th, th, thth, th, th, thth"* sound, as I ran my toe against the spinning spokes. And then, in an instant, I was on the ground, the outside of my left ankle bleeding, my tights torn and in more pain than I had ever experienced. The wheel had pulled my foot into the spokes which flipped my body instantly off the bike and threw me to the ground. My mom scooped me up into her arms and ran me to a neighbor's house and then she promptly fainted.

My mom was acutely aware of her inability to handle major injuries. She could always get us to safety just as she fainted. Learning when to ask for help is one of the critical lessons my mom tried to teach me. I still struggle with this concept. My mom mastered the art of staying conscious just long enough to get help.

My mom's friend rushed us to the hospital. A few funny things stand out about that incident. I remember my neighbor gave me a glass of Pepsi to drink in the car to get my mind off the pain. I had never had Pepsi, and for that matter, I don't think I had ever had pop. The newness was indeed a distraction. I remember sitting in the emergency room waiting room trying to put my foot into the bucket of ice water. I couldn't decide if it was more painful to have my injured foot in the ice or out of the ice. My brother and dad arrived in the emergency room and my brother brought me a package of Chuckle's candy. Candy was a rarity. Being given candy magnified the severity of the situation. It's funny the things you remember in a crisis.

I wore a cast on my leg for many weeks after the fascination of sound and vibration caused the accident. I remember my dad had to be my nurse and care for the wound every day. A removable square had been cut out of the cast where my ankle was for my dad to tend to my wound. Although my dad is a wonderful nurse, I remember feeling sick to my stomach and having so much pain when he would treat the wound every day with the hydrogen peroxide and ointment. For years—and even today—the scar stands as a reminder (almost my own version of curiosity killed the cat) of how all actions have consequences.

I got to sit in bed for days watching TV. I remember quickly getting bored with TV and flipping through Japanese cartoon books. Although TV was an unusual activity for our family, watching old home movies on the projector was a favorite pastime of our family. We always ate homemade popcorn as we watched the movies, too. I clearly remember watching my brother and me sword fight with paper swords, wearing paper bags as armor and homemade paper hats.

On the screen we fought valiantly, but occasionally I would wander towards the camera crying. I never liked losing. Even though I have no memory of the actual paper sword fight in the movie, I could always sympathize with the little Kayla in that home movie.

The movies were soundless, other than the sound of the projector, but in my mind I filled in the words. Some were clear, "Dddddaaaaadddddyyyyy" as I wiped my crying eyes with outstretched hands towards the camera; others were simply imagined.

My mom was in remission when moved to Japan. She took a regimen of medications prescribed by a Japanese doctor who saw her on base. Over time the doctor left the base and a new doctor took over. Her medications were changed and the cancer came back. She was certain the Hodgkin's disease had returned, but her new doctors were convinced it was breast cancer. She was right, and they were wrong. A Japanese woman in her life made her a thousand origami cranes. The ancient Japanese legend promises that anyone who folds a thousand origami cranes will be granted one wish. She wished for my mom's health. I still have the thousand cranes, which remind me of the generous spirit of the Japanese people.

Chapter 4
San Mateo, California (1972)

We were transferred to America when I was nearly five years old. We moved to California and suddenly no one noticed me. It was quite a shock when every other kid had blonde hair, and I discovered I was simply ordinary. I walked the streets of San Mateo without fanfare. I blended into the crowd. I adjusted just fine to no longer being photographed, stared at and touched by strangers. I am pretty sure those four years in Japan attributed to my distaste for being photographed even today.

My mom was no longer in remission. We were transferred urgently to California so my mom could go through experimental treatments at Stanford University, because Hodgkin's disease at the time was one hundred percent fatal. Going through the experimental treatment was a gamble, but her fate would have been sealed without them.

The only problem with our planned transfer was that I had recently gotten over a mild case of chickenpox and I had passed a severe case of it onto my brother. As we prepared for our international flight, we had all our transfer papers ready, our pets were vaccinated and Kevin was covered head to toe in the chickenpox. Our transfer home was crucial to my mom's health. So, my parents decided to have Kevin travel home as if he was a make-believe robber wearing a ski mask. He even wrote in Crayola on his suitcase, "I am a robber." This plan was working just fine until somewhere over the Pacific Ocean a stewardess noticed the speckled little boy on the plane.

Shortly after arriving in San Francisco, our little family, animals and of our belongings were ushered out of the city limits to a hotel for quarantine. While we were quarantined, officials attempted to verify that Kevin indeed only had chickenpox and was not the carrier of some unknown deadly foreign disease.

I had no previous good memories of life in America to call my own, and I was not encouraged as our arrival seemed abrupt and unwelcoming. I continued to think that many things about America were odd for a while. I had never seen such perfect little yards with high wooden fences before. Other kids told me I spoke very good English for being Japanese. I didn't understand that comment since I thought it was obvious that I wasn't Japanese. After all, my blonde hair was the stark contrast to my former neighbors in Japan.

Cancer Treatment, Another Pet, Hospital Games

After the brief quarantine was over, family friends had taken Kevin and me into their home while he healed and my mom started cancer treatments. Soon I started kindergarten, the animals learned their way around the new neighborhood and my mom started a cocktail of experimental doses of chemotherapy and radiation.

She was treated with a variety of medications at Stanford University. One of them was steroids to help deal with the side effects of the other drugs. The steroids made my mom feel like she could conquer the world. Once she was so amped up, she thought getting a dog would be an excellent idea. After all, she only had to fight cancer, raise two kids and be a wife! With two cats already—why not add a dog to the mix? Kevin had been begging for a dog. One day, we visited the dry cleaners and saw a sign for free puppies. The owners of the dry cleaners had two puppies in their office.

I remember choosing our dog as we sat between two puppies. One appeared to be a small black peppy fuzz ball and the other a big black lazy fuzz ball. We picked the smaller alert puppy. We named him Tora, meaning tiger, from the Japanese war call, "Tora, Tora, Tora." Smokey was an old grumpy little cat for as long as I can remember. He wasn't fond of Tora, but Puffy was more than happy to have another creature to raise. Puffy had a mothering instinct and saw no difference between raising a human and raising a dog.

Tora was the light side of my mom's illness. The cancer was the dark and scary side. I cuddled up to Puffy and we prayed hard together for my mom. I gained a fear of separation from my mom that I had never had before. I sought comfort from my Puffy, my cat and best friend. With the addition of Tora to our furry family, our family was complete.

Whenever my mom was in the hospital, we made regular pilgrimages to see her. Even when she wasn't confined to the hospital, she was often bed ridden or sick. I formed a sideways view of mom, therefore I was quite shocked at her actual height whenever she did rise from bed.

We spent as much time in the hospital waiting room as most children spend at playgrounds. Being the rambunctious children we were, Kevin and I easily entertained ourselves for hours on end. Only when we were being naughty did we care when our dad would reappear from behind closed doors. We had a system of watching out for him so that we would never get caught disobeying his command to "behave." When we heard a door squeak, as our mom's door did, we would drop everything. By the time our dad could reach the waiting room, we would be found coloring or playing a quiet game of tic-tac-toe.

The waiting room was filled with action accompanied by a painful silence. I watched groups of people, including families, doctors and nurses as they stood or sat in corners around the room, whispering. Their words vanished into the walls. Only faint remnants of their conversations reached my ears. I was particularly fascinated by this queer feeling, yet I never understood it. Kevin seemed to understand everything; I was in awe of his age and his seemingly superior understanding of what baffled me.

I had no idea what my mom's treatments entailed, except that she was losing her hair. She also spent less and less time with us. My dad explained that she was weak, and needed her sleep to gain strength. Even after many days of sleep, however, she never seemed strong when I visited her.

Since Mom was resting most days, and Dad was often with her, Kevin and I met a lot of people at the hospital. The nurses, dressed in white, wore shoes that squeaked as they walked. We could hear them coming out from behind the big round desk in the hallway. A fast squeak towards us usually indicated that we were being too loud. Any other squeak told us that we could continue on with our games. The halls were filled with doctors that smelled of soap. Some of the doctors wore green pajamas while others wore big white coats. Mom's room was visited by many doctors.

Kevin and I met all these people. They would squat down to our heights and lower their tones. They spoke what seemed to me to be nonsense, most of which I never grasped. Sometimes new words joined my vocabulary after they had left. I used this newly acquired knowledge to chat with other people who came to the waiting room. I told one stranger my mom had chemotherapy, that cancer was in her system, and the doctors say she may never come home. He told me to wipe the smile from my face and left the waiting room.

We were confined to the waiting room by dad's orders to "wait here." This confinement was the most painful of experiences for us. My mom had told us to listen to dad and so we did. Fortunately, some days he would forgot to give the "wait here" command. On those days, we roamed the hallways. They were massive and were filled with voices calling doctors and nurses through the ceiling. The floors were shiny and slick. Sometimes, I would lie on my back and Kevin would spin me round and round by my feet on the floor. When I pleaded with him to stop, he would let go and I would skid with great enthusiasm into the wall.

One day, an old woman in a wheelchair coaxed me towards her. She wore purple, my favorite color at the time. Kevin was shy and beckoned me to come back to him. But I kept going towards her, fascinated by her presence. I had never encountered life at such a deathly state, and was compelled to touch her wrinkled and bruised arms. As I approached her, I became frightened by the overwhelming smell of urine that surrounded her. Once I got close enough, she grabbed me by the arm and wouldn't let go. Her fingers felt like what I imagined uncovered bones would feel, hard, sharp and piercing. I panicked and breathlessly screamed. A nurse answered my frightened yelps and freed me.

After that incident, I was more apprehensive about leaving the waiting room. But Kevin could convince me to do anything. Whenever he would tell me to come with him, I would follow him into the dreaded hallway. I never wandered toward an open door or to the outstretched arms of a stranger, however.

We only got caught by dad once outside the waiting room. We were sending echoes down the hallway and listening for their quick return. My dad was furious and apologized profusely to whoever was in the open doorway. The redness of his face showed under the bright lights of the hallway. We were ashamed of hurting him. He wouldn't speak to us, and his silence made me cry. Even my crying didn't break his silence.

We left the hospital and quietly crawled into the car. At home, dad seated himself in his favorite chair with a pipe in hand. Kevin and I busied ourselves in the kitchen. Since Kevin was taller he chose our frozen dinners. I was on the short side, and so I turned on the oven. Dinner would take forty-five minutes, so we set the timer and joined dad in the living room.

"What's for dinner?" Dad asked, breaking the silence.

"Hungry Man turkey, mashed potatoes and gravy, green beans and apple cobbler," Kevin announced with pride.

"Why is mom always in the hospital?" I blurted out with Puffy dangling from my arm.

Dad's expression let me know it wasn't the proper time to bring up such a question.

He gave me a long hard stare, "Your mom has cancer."

I already knew that, I just didn't understand what cancer meant. The look on my face prompted dad to go on, "Cancer is inside your mom, and it may kill her, but she is fighting to stay alive."

That was all I wanted to know. I still didn't understand, so I just assumed cancer was what was taking her hair, her color and her energy. I knew very little about death, except what I had learned of Jesus' death. I had been taught to rejoice because he will come again—and I had decided if mom died, she would come again too.

As I understood more about my mom's illness, I felt a new sense of responsibility was placed upon me. My dad brought us into my mom's room the following day. The stark whiteness of the room blinded me upon entrance. My eyes jumped around the room to find the familiar yellow roses by her bedside. I found comfort in their presence.

Mom was lying in a bed facing the door. The remaining strands of her red hair were pulled back into a ponytail. She was surrounded by large machines that reached out and joined her body. Her arms were pierced by several needles, which led to tubes that were attached to bags of fluid. My mom looked small and pale, and her eyes seemed tired.

She looked up and smiled at us. With her smile we ran into her arms, and I began to cry.

"I love you," I whispered into her ear.

She squeezed me tighter, yet her grip was still weak. Not a word was spoken of her health. Instead we discussed school, our pets and things like brushing our teeth. My mom bloomed with life, animation and laughter in our conversation. I loved her laughter. She was most alive in her laughter. I didn't want to leave her side. Time passed quickly, and before we were prepared to say goodbye, the nurse would shuffle us out of the room. My mom always looked as though she was saying goodbye forever.

Later in the week, when my dad got off work, we returned to the hospital. This time we were asked to stay in the waiting room. Kevin and I placed ourselves comfortably into our favorite chair. We shared it and sat in respectful silence for a moment. Like most young children though, we began to laugh within minutes.

A young woman joined us in the waiting room. She sat across from us and smiled. She didn't wear the face of the other people who had joined us over time. Instead, she seemed happy and at ease. She looked as if she believed in laughter, as Mom did. I took a liking to her instantly. I shouldn't have stared, and I knew it. But I was fascinated by her. I watched as she pulled candy from her purse, piece by piece. Kevin nudged me so I looked away. I felt her glaze come upon me and looked back at her.

She inquired, "Would you like a piece?"

Kevin whispered in my ear, "Ask her if it is poisoned."

And so I did.

She replied quite simply, "No."

And so we ate some.

As I was chewing, I heard my dad's voice coming around the corner. I heard wheels rolling and knew Mom was with him. Her stretcher echoed down the hallway. Looking at her lying in the bed, with nurses pushing carts connected to tubes that punctured her body, I searched her for a shadow and found none. The whiteness of the sheets had eaten her shadow, and the dark rings around her eyes had grown since the last time I had seen her.

I became painfully aware of the piece of candy melting on my tongue. I wanted to hide it, but it was too late. We were already at my mom's side. Automatically we had crawled up onto the stretcher to hug and kiss her. She was on her way to another test, but we snagged a moment with her. From behind came the sweet voice of the woman in the waiting room. Between her laughter she told Mom about the *poisoned candy*. My mind raced, I knew we were doomed.

The phrase, "Never take candy from a stranger" echoed in my ears. My eyes met Kevin's as we prepared our stories.

Much to my surprise, the lady's laughter was matched by the intensity of my mom's laughter. Mom's eyes filled with love as she squeezed us tight. Then I began to realize that it was the two of us wrapped in her arms that was willing her to live.

Family Members On the Go

I have fond memories of when my cousin Colleen, who was closer to my mom's age than mine, would come to stay with us. She taught me that walk signs meant walk to other people, but that they were a secret signal to me to run. She got me pondering about what other things had double meanings.

I remember when she visited us in California. We were looking at pictures from when she had visited us in Japan. In one photo, I am sitting in front of the Buddha crying. Colleen told me the story about what had happened when that photo was taken. She was carrying me down the inside staircase of the Buddha, and she fell. The two of us tumbled down the stairs together. That incident explained my irrational fear of stairs. Every time I walked past them, I would always feel like I was falling. Colleen suffered lingering nerve pain for the rest of her life from our fall.

At one point during my mom's long course of treatments, Kevin was sent to Montana for the summer to hang out with Joyce's family. Joyce had been one of my mom's closest friends when we lived in Japan. I was jealous of the fun that I imagined he was having, but it turned out, he was jealous I got to stay home with Mom. Being away from my sick mom filled him with more anxiety than being home to see how she was doing.

Later that summer, we drove to pick Kevin up and he was somber. It was the opposite of what any of us were expecting. I had developed an irrational fear of men with red faces and Joyce's husband had a red face sometimes. I have no memory of what caused my fear, but I feared him when he drank and his face turned red. My mom later regretted sending Kevin away during her illness. She wanted to spare him from seeing her sick, but he wanted to be home with her.

As my mom got better and stronger, my dad began to travel for his job. On one occasion as we drove to pick him up from the airport, we discovered a stow-away. In the whirlwind of haste caused by rushing into the car, we didn't notice that Puffy was sun-bathing and sleeping on our 1972 Plymouth Scamp's warm black vinyl roof. She must have been startled as she awoke to a car that was traveling through the neighborhood.

Inside the car no one noticed that Puffy was on the roof—least of all my mom, who was focused on getting to the airport as quickly as possible. On top of the car, Puffy's long hunters' claws sunk deep into the vinyl roof.

Outside, the wind whipped Puffy's face as she clung for life, using up the first of her nine lives. My brother and I were caught up in our own lives as only children can be. We were still unaware of Puffy's stow-away status and the terror that must have gripped her.

As we came to a stoplight just before my mom pulled onto a busy road, Puffy pulled her body forward, peered her frantic face down to the windshield and let out a loud distinct meow. Once Puffy made her presence known, my mom immediately pulled over and rescued Puffy, placing her into safety on the inside of our car.

I will never forget the look on Puffy's face as she sought out her people to rescue her. She laid no blame on us for accidentally putting her life in danger. She found great comfort in my arms as her heart stopped racing and her meows melted into purrs. We were best friends after all.

What has always struck me is how she went from basking in the sun to clinging for her very life on the roof of a speeding car without any warning. I was only beginning to see how true it is that sometimes we are in the brightest moment dancing, in the glory of our lives, when suddenly it feels as if the rug was pulled out from underneath us.

During my first year of kindergarten, we were still in California. We lived just down the street from my school, George Hall Elementary. My mom was quite sick and unable to walk me to school. So, I walked to school with the boy next door. He wore a patch over his left eye, and unbeknownst to the rest of the world, I couldn't see out of my left eye.

I am sure you have heard the saying "the blind leading the blind." This expression was quite literally the case for the two of us. It wasn't until I was half way through my second attempt at kindergarten that I was diagnosed as legally blind in my left eye. (Yes, it is true; I failed kindergarten.)

In actuality, the school was just down the street on the left. We would be casually walking, and walk right past the school. Neither of us noticed, nor were we worried about finding the school. We just kept walking; our parents had told us we couldn't miss it so we figured it was just ahead. Calls to our parents were a regular occurrence to see why we were absent. Our parents could walk in a straight line and find us. We never even knew that we had been lost.

Puffy was in the habit of walking with me to school too, but she didn't care where we were going as long as we were going together. She would walk me to school and then hunt in the area until it was time to walk me home. Sometimes she just went home on her own and waited for me.

The Unnamed New Addition

During our short stint in San Mateo, my parents decided to let us have a rabbit. Being an animal lover and a dreamer, I dreamed about owning a horse, raccoon and rabbit, in that order of preference. Despite the rabbit joining our home out of the order of my dreams, I was thrilled. We had a rabbit for such a short time, that we never named her. Whether or not it was a she or he is still up for debate. She was black and white. To me, she was obviously very feminine with her delicate little features. My brother believed the rabbit was a boy. This controversy played a major role in her remaining nameless.

The debate was short-lived because one day we came home to find *her* dead in the backyard. She had escaped from the safety of her container and eaten pellets of snail poisoning. And so it was that our nameless rabbit was put to rest in our backyard.

My brother wanted to share the news of our family tragedy with all the neighbors. Because we were in mourning, Kevin made a sign to place in our front yard to inform all knew and loved our nameless rabbit to mourn with us. He painstakingly wrote, "The rabbit is dead" and placed the sign by the mailbox; after all, the mailman might have wanted to offer his condolences too.

My parents were unaware of the sign out front until a neighbor congratulated my mom for being pregnant with a third child, which thoroughly confused her since she wasn't pregnant. She asked the neighbor what had given her that idea. The neighbor pointed out the sign out front which stated, "The rabbit is dead." At the time that phrase was often used in movies and TV shows to announce that a character was pregnant. Thank God for my mom's sense of humor.

Mom and Dad Behind the Wheel
My mom had a great sense of humor about everything except driving, parking and being lost. Maybe it was because she learned to drive later in life. Maybe it was because of her obsession with maps and knowing exactly where we were at all times. Or maybe it was the Achilles heel in her personality. I am certain that I witnessed my mom lose her temper inside the confines of our cars more than any other location in life. And we spent a lot of time in cars.

My mom transformed from superwoman to an ordinary person behind the wheel of her car. Sometimes she drove through our hometowns as if she was in a bumper car derby. She was always on high alert, as was I, and somehow her state of mind made her forgetful and easily disoriented. On one occasion she drove away from the gas pump while still pumping gas. She would go into a full tilt panic if she was lost, and she become unreasonable if she had to parallel park her car. I was so relieved when I was old enough to drive. I would often kick her out of the driver's seat to parallel park her car for her.

On the other hand, my dad was most at home behind the wheel of a car. He actually daydreamed of one day becoming a school bus driver. It was as if Dr. Jekyll and Mr. Hyde were my chauffeurs through life. But once my mom was in the passenger seat with a map, and my dad in the driver's seat, life would balance out. At least all was well until we were hours into a trip and trying to find our final location. That is when my brother and I would start fighting in the backseat about who was on whose side. My parents would also start fighting in the front seat about where to turn. Our mostly peaceful family antics would turn to war tactics in the final few miles of a long trip.

Chapter 5
Desoto, Texas (1972–1976)

When my mom's Hodgkin's disease went into remission again, our family was transferred to Desoto, Texas. We had two cars, three pets, two kids and two adults who needed to get from California to Texas. My parents hitched our second car up and towed it across the country with the pets in it. Naturally I was fretful and worried about our pets' safety in the towed car.

I watched from the back window as we crossed the miles. Sometimes my mom drove and sometimes my dad did, but in the pet vehicle, Puffy drove the entire way. Puffy stood in the driver's seat with her front paws on the steering wheel and stared back at me the whole time. Smokey sat in the passenger seat sometimes with his paws on the dash and other times curled up asleep. Tora sat in the middle of the back seat just like the child he was. Tora was still a young puppy.

Smokey didn't like change. He howled the entire way. We could see his complaints clearly, but thankfully, we couldn't hear him. He did make sure at least one person heard his complaints. Once when we stopped at a gas station to fill up the towing car Smokey paced back and forth across the front seats. At one point, he threw his whole body against the steering wheel causing a sudden loud honk. The attendant pumping our gas jumped out of his skin. He hadn't even noticed the animals and was stunned when our towed car noisily came to life.

We arrived in Desoto at the home my parents had pre-purchased. The green shag carpet inside stood out in sharp contrast to the brown grass surrounding our house as the sun faded away over West Lake Drive upon our arrival. We unloaded the animals first to allow them time to investigate the house while we unloaded the car. The house had been vacant awaiting our arrival.

As we toured our new home, we heard a loud yowl coming from the kitchen. We raced in to find Puffy facing off with a scorpion as her nose began to swell. Puffy had taken on the scorpion and lost. Quickly my dad unhitched the other car while my mom searched the phone book frantically for a vet. We raced her to an emergency vet where she used up life number two of her nine lives.

Our move had transpired in the middle of my first kindergarten year. But life was easy in kindergarten. Your mom packed you lunch, friends were easy to make, nap time was scheduled and crayons were always nearby. Well, I should say, most moms pack the lunches. In our house, my mom wanted to teach us independence so we packed our own lunch—even in kindergarten. I showed up to school with a bag of jalapeños, a granny smith apple and a hunk of blue cheese. I had strange tastes, even as a child. No one ever stole my lunch.

Making friends was easy for me too. On the first day at my new school I saw a little girl sitting alone on the steps.

I walked over and sat down beside her and asked, "Do you want to be my friend?"

She replied, "Yes."

And so Jennifer became my best friend while I lived in Desoto, Texas. We were total opposites, but we enjoyed a great kindergarten friendship. I was fluctuating between being a tomboy and a sissy. My favorite colors changed repeatedly. Some days I loved purple and pink with all my heart. Other days I loved green and blue with a passion. Jennifer was flexible enough to stay my friend whether I was being a sissy or a tomboy. She didn't care that my favorite color fluctuated either.

Puffy's Prey and Mom's Fear
Puffy was a tomboy through and through. She was a great hunter and settled in quite nicely to our new home. Even though she was a medium-sized sleek black cat who was a half-Siamese mixed breed, she believed she was a black panther. Even though we fed her well,

she went out hunting each day to bring a prize home for our family. Our home on West Lake Drive in Desoto was perched at the edge of a field teeming with wildlife that provided ample opportunities for Puffy to exercise her wild side. If Puffy carried her catch home dead, my brother and I would hold somber funerals for her prey. One day Puffy approached the house dragging a jackrabbit more than twice her size between her legs. The rabbit was huge, but since Puffy thought she was a black panther, it must have seemed tiny to her.

Often Puffy brought her mice friends home alive to play with—much to my mom's chagrin. Somehow it was always shocking that my mom, who was usually a picture of inner strength, would be standing on top of the washing machine, or hiding somewhere else as she screamed hysterically about a little mouse. My brother and I were then tasked with the job of rescuing my mom from the mice. Mice were among my mom's greatest fears. The very thought of them opened a window into irrational fear for her.

We all have fears. They are like boulders in our way, as well as the tiny pebbles that simply slow us down on the path of our goals. With concentrated effort, some fears can be tossed aside, and others conquered, but some fears require acknowledgement and respect.

Adventures with Uncle Tom

In my memory, my mom's brother Tom was fearless. My Uncle Tom Kelley served in the Navy and he visited us wherever we lived around the world. He always came bearing gifts, stories, games and laughter. I have memories of Uncle Tom in every home that I lived in as a child and young adult. My most vivid memories of him started on West Lake Drive although he was always present in our lives.

He won more card games than he lost because of his incredibly sharp mind. He memorized the cards that had been played and sometimes knew, even before I did, when I had a winning hand.

Uncle Tom had the gift of gab, as if he was born and raised in Ireland. I guess his heritage ran thick in his blood. His eyes glowed when he was recalling a story from his adventurous past. Every day sounded like the most glorious journey when he recounted it. He could make the mundane sound like it should be made into a major motion picture. When we travelled and toured with him, he walked a few steps in advance of us, as if the excitement to show us the next stop on our walking tour pulled him forward. Laughter boomed from his voice and his personality sparked from his smiling eyes.

Uncle Tom loved the most unlovable stray cats. Whenever we visited him, he had taken in at least one scraggly snarled-tooth cat to nurture and love back to health. When he came to our home, he could always be found with a cat on his lap. Even my faithful Puffy, who loved no other person but me, could not resist Uncle Tom. I didn't mind sharing Puffy with him.

If anyone in the family or if strangers needed help, Uncle Tom was the first one lending a hand. He was always poised to come to the rescue. He was my mom's big brother and my ally.

Uncle Tom was often with us at Christmas time. Kevin and I loved Christmas. We were eager with anticipation and excitement for weeks before the special day. Every year, Kevin and I practiced acting out what we would do when Christmas morning arrived. One of us would pretend to wake up first and go wake up the other one. Then, I would ride on Kevin's back while I held Puffy, and into the living room we would go. We would act out the excitement we would feel seeing all the presents Santa had brought. By the time Christmas morning arrived, we were well-versed imagining all possible scenarios based on who would wake up first and what presents might be under the tree. We even tried to plan for unexpected surprises.

One night in the midst of our practice, we heard the door jiggle. We looked to each other shocked that Santa had arrived. We were stunned that he was using the front door, and we were worried if he caught us, he would leave without dropping off our presents. With our hearts racing, we hid behind a wicker chair. The door jiggled and jiggled. It seemed Santa had a key and he was having trouble using it. I was tempted to go let Santa in. The animals were all sitting at the door waiting to see Santa too.

The thought crossed my mind, "What if the animals give our location away to Santa?"

My brother, on the other hand, was certain a robber was breaking in. He ran screaming down the hallway toward my parent's bedroom. Finally the door bursts open and in walked Uncle Tom.

"Is Uncle Tom Santa?" I wondered.

Kevin was relieved, I was puzzled and we were both in trouble for being awake long past midnight.

Uncle Tom had simply gone to Midnight Mass. And Santa did in fact come while we were sleeping.

Drenched Dreams

My kindergarten class was putting on the grandest of all Christmas programs that year. My mom could not sew. I can't sew. It is a hereditary thing. I think it has more to do with lack of patience than anything. I first learned of this hereditary inability to sew when our kindergarten class put on what we thought was the largest production of Sonny and Cher to ever take the stage. Dozens of little Chers were scheduled to hit the stage with their matching Sonnys.

The moms were given the task of sewing matching Sonny and Cher outfits. My mom hired a friend to sew my Cher outfit. We picked shiny green fabric and designed my outfit with a custom choker, big earrings and a headpiece—and ta da—I was Cher! My outfit had all the makings of a diva dress. I was so excited. I loved all things shiny and glittery—ok I have to admit it—I loved all things gaudy. In kindergarten, I would have willingly worn any of Cher's outfits to the grocery store.

When the big day came, I pranced onto stage, glowing with pride beside my Sonny. We sang, we danced and with every word we sang, my Sonny spit on my face. Literally, the louder we sang the faster the saliva flew from his mouth onto my face! I was distraught and disillusioned. *How did I get the one and only faulty Sonny?* My dreams of a Cher-like stardom were being drenched by Sonny at a very tender age. The show had to go on, but I was certain every eye in the audience was focused on our spitting duet.

I decided right then and there that I was done with stage life forever. I was humiliated. The wonder of my dress wasn't enough any longer to distract me from my woes. I had climbed onto the stage feeling beautiful and confidant, but once I was on stage with spitting Sonny, it took every ounce of courage I had to not add tears to my already drenched face.

In reality, I'm sure that no one noticed. The spit was probably not even visible from stage, let alone offstage. But my reality at the moment was different. I saw an imperfection out of my control as a fault line that destroyed everything in its path. I'm sure every parent had their eyes firmly fixated on their own child and didn't even notice as I deflated before their very eyes. Even my parents were probably enchanted with my smile that covered up my inner turmoil. But my view of reality was obscured by how I believed the actions of Sonny reflected on me.

Before the Sonny and Cher show at St. Elizabeth's, I was prepared to take center stage at any given moment. I was fearless and confident. Afterwards I shunned the stage. I believed imperfection had marred my stage presence. I believed that my image wasn't fully in my control. It is silly that just a bit of unintentional spit sprayed onto my face had impacted my confidence so completely, but it did.

Later I realized how we all allow a collection of minor incidents and major events of the past impact how we view ourselves. Past unintentional slights can touch us deeply and shake our confidence. The words, actions and treatment of someone can re-mold our image of ourselves. Sometimes those hurts cut so deep it separates us from our God-given gifts. I was terrified of public humiliation and I couldn't even remember where the roots of fear had been planted.

Stretching My Limits in the Water

One of my other great fears was swimming. When we lived in Desoto, the nearby YMCA in Oak Cliff was a big part of our lives.

The only problem was, as a little girl, I was a weak swimmer. My dad worked tirelessly with me in the pool. He was determined to build my confidence in the water and increase my endurance as a swimmer. Because of my fear, I clung to the side of the pool and pleaded with my dad to stay exactly where he was while I swam to him under water.

Most of the time, he complied and I successfully reached my goal to the safety of his arms. But he never allowed me to stay inside my comfort zone for very long.

Once I had accomplished one goal, he would step back farther away from me. I begged him to step in closer, inside my comfort zone. He patiently and lovingly encouraged me to swim out to him. I often swam towards him and fell short of my goal. When I came up for air and found him just outside my reach I would panic. He rescued me a few times, but after a while, he would stand his ground just outside my reach. I struggled, gasped for air and splashed my way over to him. Calling me a drama queen in the pool would have been putting it lightly. This scenario was repeated again and again until finally I could swim straight to his arms—minus the drama.

After a few successes, he stepped back again and the entire cycle repeated itself. It seems this went on for years, maybe it was only a summer, but in my mind, the memory is vivid and drawn out. At the YMCA, under the unrelenting Texas sun, I learned my first lessons of perseverance.

In retrospect, I think my dad was giving me some serious aversion therapy training. He made me face my fear nearly every weekend of spring and summer. He didn't just bring us swimming, but he intensely worked on my fears. Again and again, he would lure me into the deep water to have underwater tea parties. I was a sucker for tea parties and was willing to face down any fear to do anything my beloved dad asked of me. We spent hours underwater having tea.

Every summer I took swimming lessons at the YMCA. I was repeatedly held back from graduating to the next level because of my failure on the diving board. Each time I stood on the diving board, I stared down into the vast shiny blue surface below me with no concept of how long it would take me to convert from free falling through the air to splashing into the water. It wasn't until later that we discovered that I simply could not see or perceive the distance.

The YMCA played a major role in my parent's discovery that I was severely visually challenged. They had taken me to the eye doctor when we lived in Japan. They repeatedly expressed concerns for my inability to recognize the people in our lives. My inability to recognize people was so bad that my brother used to try to trick me as he jumped on my bed in Japan without fear of repercussion. The scenario would play out the same every time.

Upon finding Kevin jumping on my bed I would demand, "Stop jumping on my bed, Kevin."

He would change his voice and innocently proclaim, "I am not Kevin. I am his friend, Brian. Kevin is outside and he told me I could jump on your bed."

I would then stomp out of my room, head out the backyard in search of Kevin to scold him for letting his friend jump on my bed. Yeah, it was that bad.

One day my mom brought me to swimming lessons late. My class was already in the water. She sent me to join my class while she waited beside the pool in a chair. I walked all the way around the pool and back to where I had left my mom.

"My class is not here," I whined.

Pointing she said, "They are right there in the corner of the pool in the deep end."

I trudged back out around the pool while looking in earnest for my class.

I returned to her side insisting, "No, they are not here. We must be here on the wrong day."

My mom walked me to my class and promptly made another eye doctor appointment. I clearly remember the day I got my new glasses. The eye doctor was in a strip mall just across the street from my school. I remember arriving at school with my mom and being in awe of the world around me. I had never known I went to school in a brick building and that there were actually lines between the bricks. I stared in wonder at the pink bricks with mortar in between each one. And then I noticed the trees. I did not know trees have individual leafs. I thought they were big green blobs. It was awe inspiring.

My new glasses didn't help me when I swam, though. Over the summer, we often went swimming in large man-made lakes in Texas. They seemed enormous; the squishy, muddy bottoms only added to my apprehension. At one lake we would swim across the seemingly gigantic body of water toward three towering diving-boards. My heart raced in fear as we swam the entire length of the lake anticipating the jumps I would be asked to make. I never thought to refuse my dad's requests to join him, despite the tremendous amount of fear I was experiencing.

Several things scared me about diving from these boards. They were incredibly tall. That was enough to cause me fear, but with my severe vision problems, my eyes told my brain I was jumping into an endless pit. I was unable to see the water below me from any height. I had to trust completely in my dad. The climb to the top was extremely long. I knew I was very, very high in the air. I also had a fear of falling, coupled with a fear of being under water. These fears caused me to tremble from head to toe as I climbed from one rung of the stairs to the next.

As a child, I never fully conquered this fear. Each and every time I climbed those stairs, I trembled, my breath was caught short, my feet itched, my head spun and I'd throw up just a little in my mouth. And yet, there always was a next time. I guess you could say I did, in a way, defeat this fear because I never allowed it to paralyze me. I always pushed onward despite my physical and emotional reaction. Even now, when I experience fear, I see myself as a girl facing down the sensation, moving onward and upward despite it.

A Reward Reveals Racism

I was often rewarded for my bravery. When I was in kindergarten my mom took me to the store and told me I could buy any doll I wanted. I remember it so clearly. We weren't big shoppers, so it was a huge deal to go to the store to buy a doll. I stood in each aisle searching their faces looking for the most beautiful and lovely doll of them all. Finally, I saw her. I fell immediately in love and proudly left the store to take her home.

Sometime after my delightful new purchase my mom and I headed to downtown Dallas on a public bus toward Neiman Marcus. I sat on the bus contently playing with my beloved doll. Soon I noticed my mom pulling me in close. I snuggled up enjoying the affection. Later, I realized she wasn't really releasing her grip. *What was wrong?*

As I looked around the bus, I noticed the angry faces of several of the adults around me. I was troubled and puzzled as they glared at me with hatred and contempt. I, with my blonde hair, my mom a red head and my little black baby doll sat silently on the bus. When we departed the bus, my mom explained prejudice to me for the first time.

I had lived most of my life in the bubble of a military base in Japan. I was accustomed to all colors, races and multiple language speakers living cohesively together. I didn't know there was racial hatred in the world. I never realized I could be openly despised for loving my darling black baby doll.

On the way home on the bus, I sat defiantly with my beautiful doll lovingly in my arms. I wasn't going to back down or change my views based on the angry adults around me. I loved my doll, and the opinion of the others wasn't going to take away my love.

I still have fond memories of playing with my baby doll. My favorite recollection is that my brother thought I really believed she could talk. I carried on endless conversations with her, all of which I knew were pretend, but my brother thought I was serious. I loved to talk to her, even though she never talked back, but even more I loved listening to my brother try to talk sense into me. There was a certain mischief in it filled me with glee—something similar to the joy I took in being defiant on the bus with racists.

Tea Parties, Perfume and Studying Cats At My Table

Shortly after I got my doll, my Uncle Tom gave me a little child's table for Christmas. I loved my table. It was perfectly square, had yellow legs and was solid enough for me to sit on top of. I had tea parties with my stuffed animals, Puffy and my doll, at that table. I wrote, "Puffy is love" on the underside in crayon.

One Christmas, I was given a chemistry set and perfume set. I converted my table into a work bench. It was at my table that I created my very first perfume. Over time I created a lot of perfumes there, but it was my first one that I loved the most. I thought it was elegant. I must have been about seven years old when I created that perfume, but the scent memory of it has lingered with me through the years.

Puffy and I had tea parties, explored chemistry and wrote journals at my table. I wonder if someplace in the world there is a little solid table that still says, "Puffy is love" on the bottom side.

I also sat at the table and read my favorite cat book again and again. I learned about cat breeds, cat caretaking tips and other fun tidbits about cats. I studied it, read it and re-read it through the years. After much study, I decided that some day when I grew up and could get any cat I wanted in the world, I would get an Abyssinian cat. It has all the qualities I admired and loved so much about Puffy.

Tora, the Dashing Dog

By learning about cats and having them as pets, I found cats to be much smarter than dogs. My dog, Tora, like any other dog, loved to hang his head out of the window as we drove. I have absolutely no idea what possessed him to jump out of the window, but he did it one evening as we were driving home at about 45 miles per hour from the YMCA. One minute the wind was blowing in our faces, and in the next, he had launched out of our laps through the window and onto the road. Our eyes never left Tora's body as he spun in circles on the road in an upright semi-sitting position. My dad was furious.

In retrospect, I think he responded more out of fear than anger as he pulled the car onto the side of the road, jumped out and dodged the traffic to retrieve Tora. Miraculously, every speeding car had missed hitting Tora as he spun across the road. Tora was stunned. He never jumped out of the window again.

Much of our lives were lived outdoors with these three black furry spectators, Tora, Puffy and Smokey. The pets did their thing and we did our thing, but they always had a watchful eye on us. Sometimes we played as a unit and sometimes it was just me and Puffy against the world. It just depended on the day. We spent countless hours hiking, exploring and camping in the wilderness of Texas. The cats had to stay home when we camped, since we had not as a family elevated to the level of weirdness I aspired to, but Tora always came along—rain, shine, sleet or snow.

Tora was an outdoorsman's dream dog. He was game to try anything at least once and was mostly fearless if we were all together. Occasionally, his willingness to follow us anywhere got Tora in trouble. Sledding and hiking in the snow was a favorite pastime for our family.

On one trip we crossed Ten Mile Creek using a log as a bridge. Tora was hip-hopping through and above the snow the entire way and did not follow us out onto the log. Instead, Tora ran out onto the frozen river, lost his footing and began to slowly slide out into the deeper portion of the river. He looked to us in terror, not daring to move beyond a lifted eyebrow. We could see the river moving fast below the thin layer of ice Tora was perched on.

We all called and called and called Tora. He was frozen with fear. My dad inched his way out toward Tora calling him gently to come to him. As my dad approached, Tora leapt toward my dad just as the ice below his feet gave way. In an instant, Tora went through the ice and was under water. My dad transformed into a superhero as he lunged for Tora. He caught the scruff of Tora's neck before the fast moving water under the broken ice could carry him away. My dad opened his jacket, tucked Tora inside and we all traced our path back toward the house as fast as we could go. Tora was shaking from head to toe as we quickly submerged him in warm water at home. Tora grew a deeper devotion for my dad after that.

Camping and Fishing with Dad and Grandpa

Many of our outdoor adventures included water moccasins, tarantulas, bees and fishing. I loved to fish. Well, the truth was, I loved to hang out with my dad and brother, so fishing became my love. I did love catching fish, but waiting to catch fish was boring. Thankfully, my dad was a great storyteller, making up countless entertaining tales. Fishing and storytelling went hand in hand. My brother and I were often the heroes of his stories.

I wasn't always fond of fishing with other people, and maybe that is because of my Grandpa Mohs. One time, while we were visiting my grandparent's farm in Medford, Minnesota, we went on a family fishing trip. We caught a sheep head fish that day. I guess they aren't good eating fish, because it was decided we were not going to eat this fish. However, it had been mortally wounded in the process of being caught. I decided that this dead fish was my new best friend. Puffy wasn't along and I needed someone to love on. My mom put the fish in an old milk carton for me. I carried the dead fish with me all over the farm.

My granddad was quite annoyed by my parents, who were allowing me to carry a dead fish around. He argued with my mom about it, but my mom always was one to let me come to my own conclusions. She told him eventually the fish would smell and I would voluntarily relinquish my pet. My granddad was furious. I was oblivious to their disagreement and the potential odor. When I went to take a nap, I left my carton with my fish outside. It was, in fact, starting to smell. When I woke up I found an empty milk carton. I searched the farm and sat down to cry. My mom knew exactly what had happened and confronted my grandpa. He was unashamed of his actions and angry that I was crying. I never trusted him again.

Our favorite campsite in Texas was in Meridian State Park. We had a ritual of activities we always did there. Once the tent went up, I had a dozen things on my agenda. I wanted to check the lake for water moccasins, take Tora on the slide and swings at the playground with me and climb the sheer shale limestone cliffs with my dad, Kevin and Tora. After all that, I was ready to frolic through the flowery fields of Texas Blue Bonnets, followed by a hike to the cliffs. Once we were there, we could steal chunks of honeycomb from bees' nests and then eat the waxy honey delight.

We always joked that Tora must have been half goat. He was able to scramble up the sheer cliffs faster than us like a mountain goat. Tora was part poodle, Lhasa Apso and cocker spaniel. Lhasa Apso is small breed of mountain wolf from Tibet and we could see that side of him clearly as we climbed. As the sun would set, we would huddle around the camp fire, listen to my parents tell scary stories and watch the sparks of fire float away into the dark sky.

Capturing Critters

Often the outdoors collided with the indoors, much to my mom's dismay. My brother and I loved to capture critters outdoors and bring them into our bedrooms at night. Our favorite creatures included fire flies and tadpoles. Fireflies were surprisingly easy to catch. We would grab them with glass jars and poke holes into the top so they could breathe. I loved going to sleep with the blinking patterns of fireflies going off in the jar beside my bed. Despite the air holes, I always awoke to find my fireflies dead in the morning. I liked to believe they were simply sleeping. I would take them back outside to be free, but I'm quite certain I was only setting them free to decompose outside rather than by my bedside.

We also captured countless tadpoles, which were surprisingly fast. We brought them inside and enjoyed watching them as their bodies changed. Their transformation seemed to take forever, until one night, they must have turned into frogs overnight, because we woke to find no tadpoles left in our bedrooms. I still wonder where those frogs went.

We hunted for our tadpoles in the West Lake, which was the lake that defined our street. One a particularly stormy night, we lost the lake. A lightning strike broke the dam which held our lake. When morning came, I found a creek in an empty lakebed. The storm went on. My mom wouldn't let us out to explore until the next day. I stared out the window and dreamed of dancing along the shoreline and fishing.

When the storm passed, my mom let us out in rubber rain boots and a raincoat which glistened in the dampness. We slushed around in the fresh mud surrounding us. A club was formed that day of all the neighborhood boys and me: The Serpent Club. In the next year that followed the big storm, we swarmed the vacant lot looking for everything, anything and nothing.

In the deserted basin of West Lake, I learned about the past through fossils and arrowheads. I watched as life inhabited the empty field, and grass grew fresh and green between my toes. The barn that once sat beside the lake looked lonely without its shore. The year I moved, the barn burned down before the teary eyes of the Serpent Club.

Puffy is Missing

Puffy, an indoor and outdoor cat, loved the change in her hunting grounds. She wandered the vacant fields around our home to hunt wildlife to bring her prey home to me. Even as she enjoyed her outdoor adventures, she was always home by dark. One night though, much to our surprise, she didn't show up.

We searched the streets calling, "Here kitty, kitty, kitty!"

We expected her to run up to us at any moment. Instead, at nearly seven years old, I went to bed for the first time since I was two without my constant companion.

The next day, first thing in the morning, I ran to the back door expecting her to be sitting by the door crying to come in, but she wasn't there. Again we searched the neighborhood all day and night looking for Puffy with no luck. The next morning, again, I ran to the back door expecting her to be there. She wasn't there. This pattern repeated for days. I was heartbroken. My parents led many search parties. One night they told me it had been too long. I had to accept that she was never going to be there at the backdoor or anywhere at all. It was a truth too difficult for me to bear.

Each morning I couldn't help myself; I looked expectedly out the backdoor in hopes of a miracle. Finally, on the day I had promised myself that would be the last day I would hope to find her, her broken body was lying on the cement porch. She was very obviously injured, but Puffy was alive. She lifted her head and purred as I dropped to my knees to greet her. She was unable to stand up. I was overjoyed to see her and ran to wake my parents with the news. When we came back, she attempted to lift her broken body off the concrete, but she could only get her two front legs below her.

We rushed her to the vet with great care. The x-ray showed her diaphragm had been torn and all of her organs were pressing against her heart. The vet preformed emergency surgery. He determined she had been hit by a car on the day that she had vanished. She had dragged her broken body home with her two front feet. She had chosen not to go off and die, but instead to trust and return to her family. With dogged determination and perseverance, she came home.

Puffy trusted that getting home would be worth it and persevered against the odds, but life number three was taken by that car.

After her surgery, I nurtured Puffy. I pampered her with bedside tea parties of tuna and milk as she recuperated. Soon after the stitches were removed, she reentered life as fearless as she had always been.

All Dirt Patches are Not Created Equal

With Puffy recovered, we went back to camping our way across America. Our travels brought us to Lake Murray. It turned out to be a memorable campsite in Oklahoma that changed the way I viewed things. It had seemed like a perfectly good place to pitch a tent in the daylight hours. In Oklahoma, one patch of dirt appeared just as good as the next patch of dirt. We went about the business of making an outdoor temporary home with practiced ease and proficiency.

When night fell, we already had our fire burning, full bellies and were ready for a relaxing evening of storytelling around the campfire. We stared into the fire, laughed, told scary stories and eased into the comfort of the familiarity of each other's companionship. It was just then, when we felt most at ease, that one of us noticed the ground was moving. It wasn't just a random creature or the wind blowing kind of movement. Instead, the entire ground around us was shifting and moving.

My dad reached for a flashlight to illuminate our curiosity. We discovered hundreds of tarantulas crawling on top and around each other at our feet. Needless to say there was some screaming going on along with, fast movements and frantic decisions to be made. We ran to our tent, leapt in and zipped the tent behind us. Once we were inside, we searched every nook and cranny of the tent and our bedding. We patted each other down to make sure no stowaways made it into the tent with us.

Once everything was secure, we peered out to the phenomena just outside our tent. We were trapped for the night in a cloth prison and our guards were the hundreds of tarantulas who stayed on duty throughout the darkness. I never again assumed one patch of dirt was as good as the next patch of dirt. I knew from then on with complete certainty that an unseen world existed below our feet.

Imaginary Lions Tamed and Unspeakable Acts Committed

When I was about eight years old, I believed wholeheartedly, without a shadow of a doubt, that a lion lived under my bed in our home. I believed it so completely that I would not walk near my bed during the day or at night. I walked the outer edges of my room. When I had to get into bed, I made a running jump from as far away as humanly possible. Once I was inside the safety zone, I sighed with relief.

My heart literally was racing whenever I had to go to bed. Thankfully, most nights my dad carried me and Puffy to bed. He never knew it, but he was slaying lions for me each time he escorted me safely through the air to the top of my bed. Sometimes, though, my dad travelled and I had to leap like a daredevil to safety when he was out of town. On those nights, Puffy was on her own to make it to bed. I needed every ounce of strength and balance to fly through the air successfully.

I remember some nights leaping out of my bed to the doorway because I was certain my lion was more active than normal. Oddly, I did not think a lion slept under my parent's bed. Sometimes I would sleep for a while on the floor next to their bed where it was safe. This lion only lived under my bed when we lived in Desoto. He did not follow us when we moved away later. I was certainly glad when we left the lion that slept under my bed in Texas. No tears were shed over him.

I will never forget the moments that surrounded my shift from being a naive child to becoming a collector of hidden fears. It happened in just one night before I started believing a lion lived under my bed, and after that night, nothing was ever the same. I very suddenly experienced a hurt and shame so deep, that it changed the course of my life. At the tender age of eight years old, a babysitter abused me. That night dragged by in inches.

My brother told my parents that he had overheard the babysitter trying to get me to take my clothes off. This was years before child molestation was part of the public conversation. In those days, sexual abuse was still quite secretive and socially unspeakable. No one knew what do back then. My parents confronted the parents and the boy the next day. During the conversation, I overheard the babysitter blame me. I took the blame to heart, and the enemy used it to confuse and disorient me.

From that period of my life onward, I could feel and sense a darkness I had never known before. From within that new darkness, I changed my direction in life onto a path leading me deeper and deeper into the wilderness. I'm sure the lion moved into my bedroom that night and hid under my bed waiting to devour me. I wrapped myself up tight in my yellow butterfly sheets, attempting to cocoon myself safely away from the consuming fear.

Would you believe I never once looked under my bed to see if there actually was a lion living under there? I just believed it with all my heart. Even though I was wrong, I was living my life around my flawed thinking. In reality, all that lived under my bed was my fear and a litter of black socks Puffy stole regularly from my dad's drawers. She treated her collected socks as if they were her kittens. She had a mothering instinct that surpassed her reality of being spayed and unable to have kittens.

Chapter 6
Munich, Germany (1976–1981)

In the summer of 1976, we moved to Munich, Germany. I remember clearly the day my dad came home from work and announced we were moving. I was eight years old. I sat in our papasan chair from Japan in our Texas living room.

My dad pulled out the globe and stuck a magnet on Texas and said, "We are here."

He spun the globe and put a magnet onto Germany and announced, "We are moving here."

We had to go to the doctor and have painful shots to get vaccinated for the move. I remember my parents filling out stacks of paperwork about each of the family members and our three pets. Our house was sold; our furniture and many possessions were packed for storage. The rest of our possessions were shipped to meet us in Germany. I remembered all the goodbyes this time. In the past, I had arrived to new places without a sense of loss.

Spared from terror

Most of all I remember eavesdropping on an anti-terrorism class. I didn't even know what terrorism was. And yet, I was learning not to stand in crowds, to avoid well-known American hangouts, and to be on the look-out for suspicious activity. I had barely just learned about prejudice and suddenly I was being trained to avoid suicide bombers. I wondered why my parents were moving us into a war zone. It was in that training the first ounce of apprehension entered my thoughts about the move. When we landed in Germany, I discovered the police carried machine guns in the airport. From then on, I was on alert and took our training seriously.

In our years overseas, we saw the devastating results of terrorism many times. Our base was under high alert regularly. All the school children often gathered on Hospital Hill while the Military Police searched our school in response of bomb threats. American hangouts, American housing, the front gates to base and the Oktoberfest were common targets for terrorist attacks.

The terrorists had often been successful and memorials stood on many of the bases we visited across Europe honoring the victims. Kidnappings were also a threat that hung over our heads. We were reminded of the danger around us by articles in *Stars and Stripes*, our main source of news.

One year, I had planned on being at Oktoberfest the day a terrorist bombed an area that Americans frequented. It turned out I wasn't in the mood, so I skipped going. I ended up sitting home alone watching re-runs of *The Lone Ranger* wondering why on earth I had decided to stay home. Then the phone rang with the distinctive buzz of an international call. I answered the phone and heard the worried voice of a friend, who informed me of the bombing. She was frantic because the S-bahn commuter rail stopped right across the street from our home. She filled my head with fears that the terrorist would jump off the S-bahn at our stop and knock on my door any minute.

Puffy and I kept a vigilant eye out for potential terrorists. No armed terrorist arrived at my doorstep and thankfully I hadn't attended his bombing location that day either. We later learned that the terrorist had died while attempting to put the bomb in place.

Surviving the Snow

We had to make many adjustments to live in Germany. After living in Texas, where if there was even a light dusting of snow on the ground, school was cancelled, I was quite excited by the first sight of snow in Munich. That year, I remember that I stood four feet four inches tall and overnight it snowed four feet six inches. I woke up delighted at the thought of a mega snow day. Much to my surprise, this snow was only the first of many to come, and school was never canceled for snow.

My mom wrapped me up in a massive down coat, goofy looking moon boots and pointed me toward school. The task of getting from home to school in snow taller than me seemed impossible. Not only could I not see in the blinding white snow that blanketed everything, but also I had never attempted to move when I was dressed like the Goodyear tire man. Step by step, I pushed my way forward until I found a tunnel created by those who had gone before me. In some places, mini avalanches threatened to bury me in a great white mound.

I could not see where I was going, but I faithfully moved forward until much to my surprise, I reached the school. The moon boots my mom had bought me, which I had never before seen a need for, became my most prized possession. The coat, hat, mittens and scarf, which all seemed excessive when my mom insisted we purchase those months before snow ever arrived, became part of my wardrobe for years to come.

When my mom said it snowed in Germany, I imagined a light dusting which blew into mini-tornados like the dust devils of Texas. She was from North Dakota, so she knew how to prepare. When I found my way to school through the wall of white, I learned two simple lessons: prepare for the unimaginable and move forward then, you will be able to reach un-seeable, seemingly unreachable goals. My moon boots were blue. It was currently my favorite color.

Puffy learned to thrive, going on adventures no matter what the weather. I, on the other hand, was freezing. I had somehow gotten it into my mind we couldn't use the heaters in the house. My parents were always frugal. I assumed we didn't have the heat on in the house because we couldn't afford it. I awoke freezing every morning. I took baths instead of showers so I could put my entire body under water except my nose. I wrapped all the animals under my blanket while I dried my hair for warmth. I got dressed under the covers. Puffy simply learned to turn on the radiator, which sat mostly unused beside my bed, on her own. I would walk into my toasty room some afternoons and find her basking in the heat. I always reprimanded her and turned off the radiator before my parents could notice this blatant waste of money. Little did I know that because our home was on base, our heat was free. Years later, I learned that I was allowed to turn on the radiator in my room whenever I wanted. Puffy was smarter than I was.

Tora loved the snow more than any other outdoor event. I'm not a dog person, but I sure was a Tora person. Puffy and I adored him like a little brother. He was game for anything as long as snow was involved. He would enthusiastically jump through the snow like a rabbit. In Germany, the snow was often deep enough for him to vanish from sight temporarily and then bounce up just high enough to clear the snow in front of him. Because of the extreme cold, he always wore a sweater to play in the snow. His black fur contrasted with his red sweater. Tora had no shame when it came to dressing up. We also put our orange ski goggles on Tora and he would just go with the flow.

My brother and I played for hours in the snow. Our favorite snow-creations were forts and igloos. The forts were for snowball fights, but the igloos were built solely for the purpose of giving Tora the opportunity to be a hero to the cats. We built strong round igloos in the front yard just the right size for Puffy, Smokey and Tora to fit into. We then would close off the igloo with the pets inside.

We would call, "Tora save the kitties, Tora save the kitties!"

And Tora would respond by bursting through the igloo walls and leading the cats out to safety. He would prance around as if he was a super hero and the cats would gratefully make a beeline for the front door.

Hiding Dad's Pipes

When we were inside in Germany, Puffy and I spent countless hours sitting on my dad's lap. Every day after work, my dad would come home and sit in his black leather chair. He smoked a pipe, drank a beer and talked to me. I would sometimes cough. When I learned about the dangers of smoking in health class, I became a constant nag to my dad. It was unbearable to me to think my dad was giving up a single day of his life for the sake of his pipe.

I started hiding his pipes from him while he was at work. He would come home ready for a smoke and a beer only to find his entire pipe collection—tobacco and all—missing. It was a game to me, yet at the same time, it was not a game at all. Most of the time, I relented and would tell him where his pipes were; but occasionally, I pushed the limits and hid them for hours forcing my nicotine-starved dad to smoke a cigarette. I would give up and give them back to him for the night.

My dad was a creature of habit. Alcohol was a major player in our home as well. My mom only drank socially, but my dad drank every day. I was twelve years old when my dad turned over a new leaf. He quit smoking and drinking and became a die-hard health food nut.

Later we learned that I was allergic to smoke. My dad felt terrible for subjecting me to smoke all those years. But I adored my dad and would have sat in a burning building to be with him. And he adored me enough to sit with me and my cat for endless hours. He would also carry Puffy and I to bed every single night until I was twelve years old. Faithfully he would give me a kiss goodnight. I always insisted he needed to give Puffy a kiss too. Every night he kissed us both and tucked us in.

Puffy's is Missing—Again

When we were living in a first-floor apartment, our upstairs neighbor threatened to report Puffy to the military police. That neighbor had a squirrel feeder on her balcony. Puffy had discovered this prime hunting spot, and simply picked off the squirrels as they ran up the wall to the feeder. We had a large squirrel bone graveyard in the dirt directly below our balcony.

I attempted to teach Puffy not to hunt the squirrels, but I was not successful. We agreed to have her declawed to stop her from killing the squirrels. Our neighbor agreed not to report Puffy. The problem was Puffy refused to be tamed. She was completely unaware of the fact that she didn't have any claws and continued hunting squirrels. Thankfully we got transferred across base into a duplex. Our new home backed up to thick woods and we created a new graveyard for her prey.

As far as Puffy was concerned, she needed to provide for her family, which included her humans, her dog Tora, her big brother Smokey, and her litter of kittens made up of my dad's black socks under my bed. She believed she was bigger than her prey, fully armed with claws and faster than any animal on earth. In reality, she was a small-to-medium sized clawless cat. There was nothing extraordinary about her size, build or physical strength. Little did she know she was handicapped in comparison to other cats. It was all in her mind. She overtook animals that were faster, bigger and stronger than her by sheer determination.

Declawing Puffy was not uneventful. When we picked up Puffy from the vet after the procedure, she had already removed both of her bandages. The vet didn't want her pulling out her stitches so he put new bandages on both paws. By the time we got home she already had one bandage off, but the other one stayed on. When we returned to the vet to have her post-op appointment, the vet had to cut the second bandage off. Inside we found an infected and swollen paw. The bandage had been too tight and she lost all the pads on her foot. Puffy wasn't pleased with the vet or us.

I soaked Puffy's infected paw in chamomile tea and applied her medicine regularly. She wasn't up to wandering the neighborhood, but she was stir crazy. We started to allow her to sit on the balcony to sunbathe and get fresh air. One day we forgot her out on the balcony and left for the day. When we returned Puffy was missing. We were a little bit worried because she was still healing. We went out into the forest that surrounded our house and started calling for her. She didn't come to us.

Our worry increased as the sun set. We walked through the forest with flash lights calling for her deep into the night. I was frantic. Puffy didn't speak German; she was Japanese after all. The next day we made signs. One read, "Lost Cat." The other was translated into German: "Verloren Katze." We plastered the base and local German neighborhoods with our signs. We rallied our friends to help us search for Puffy on foot and by bicycle. Finding Puffy became our obsession. When day after day passed with no sign of Puffy, despair set in once again.

One day we got a call from across base. Someone had found a black cat! My mom and I raced there—only to find that it wasn't Puffy. I couldn't imagine life without Puffy, but as time passed I began to think a Puffy-less reality was upon me.

Finally I came home to find my brother proudly waiting to present me with a very frightened, but thankful Puffy in his arms. He had answered a call from someone who spoke only German. They had found a terrified black cat in their yard and had trapped her in a shed. Kevin had ridden his bike to their home and carried her home to safety. Kevin was already my hero, but after that day, his status rose even higher.

Puffy used up life number four wandering lost and confused among the German Shepherds and Dachshunds that dominated the homes of our German neighbors.

Puffy Stays at School

Thankfully my fifth grade teacher let Puffy come to class so I was able to keep a close eye on her. Fifth grade was an especially educational year for me. I had to go to the Special Education Department that year. On the humiliating walk from my fifth grade homeroom down the hall to the Special Education Department, I learned the fine art of being humble. It wasn't a voluntary lesson. I didn't choose to leave my classroom every week to go to Special

Education Department. I felt it was bad enough that I wore the same military issued glasses as every other bespectacled student at school. In addition, though, I wore a thick lens that distorted my left eye.

I tried to walk casually down the hall as if I just had a bathroom pass. Once I walked past the restrooms and down the hall that only led to the Special Education Department, there wasn't much use playing it off. Normally no one said anything as I passed them going the opposite direction of my class on my solitary walk down the vast hallway. It was later when I returned to class or was at lunch when people questioned what was wrong with me. No one dared make fun of me because I had already shown that I would fight back. I had punched a boy in the nose for making fun of my friend.

I was sent to Special Education because my piano teacher noticed my eyes were not working together. I am not musically gifted in any way, shape or form, but my parents did give me the opportunity to learn music. Their hard earned money wasn't wasted, because without piano, no one would have ever noticed my eyes were sending separate messages to my brain. Thankfully, my teacher realized I wasn't just a bad piano student, but I was simply not getting information correctly from my eyes to my brain.

I never learned the piano in any significant way, but I did learn two lessons from my teacher: I could retrain my eyes and you are what you eat. My piano teacher fed her baby so many carrots that the baby took on an orange hue. My mom was never one to hold back her thoughts. She asked my teacher if she noticed her baby was orange. My piano teacher was offended. My mom never changed her ways of speaking her mind. She wasn't the first or the last person my mom managed to offend with her curiosity.

In the Special Education Department, I sat in front of an antiquated machine which rushed the words of a story past my eyes. At first I was frustrated, because I could only see a grey line, but eventually it worked. Once there was a purpose I could readily identify with, I got over the awkwardness of the situation. I let go of my pride and thrived.

In the spring of fifth grade, I finished my Special Education trips and wrote my first poem. I doubt I ever would have written without first falling in love with the sound words make when they bump up against each other in the written form.

The best part of fifth grade was at the end of most days when I returned to my classroom, Puffy was basking in the sun in the homework inbox near the window. One time when I glanced over at Puffy, I saw an elephant out the window on the playground. I remember it was a beautiful crisp cool day. My eyes continued to dance a tango between Puffy sleeping and the large grey elephant standing by the swing set.

Being aware that I was still in class, my eyes would also sweep from the teacher, down to my desk and then to a sideways glance towards the window scene of Puffy and the elephant. I really thought my imagination was playing tricks on me; I whipped my head to the left and stared out the window. Clearly I could see an elephant walking across the playground towards my classroom window. She seemed to be in no hurry and was walking directly towards me as if I was in some sort of dream sequence.

I wondered if I was having a momentary lapse from sanity—after all, elephants didn't normally visit me at school. I blinked hard to check my vision again.

While pointing towards the window I whispered, "Elephant . . ."

The class looked towards me instead.

Their eyes followed my arm and in a large collective gasp they hollered, "Elephant!"

With my sanity confirmed, my mind was able to digest the message my eyes were sending. I quickly remembered that the *Little Oktoberfest* was setting up tents on base when I walked to school. The mystery of the elephant in the playground was quickly solved after we ran to the site of the *Little Oktoberfest* hollering, "ELEPHANT!" while pointing towards our school. The handlers followed us to our playground and our visitor willingly meandered back across our school grounds towards her tent.

Defending Animals, Dressing Up Pets and Family Mealtime

I wasn't always as eloquent and subtle about other animals. I remember the day I stormed across the street carrying the neighbor's large male cat in my arms and pounded on their front door. When they answered, I proceeded to scold them for allowing their cat to come into my front yard and bully Smokey. I demanded they teach their cat to stay in their yard. The neighbors returned the favor by stomping to my front door. They had a very stern talk with my surprised parents for allowing their child to scold them.

Years later after we moved away, my parents ran into our old neighbors who were still sour about the cat-scolding incident. Honestly, if a kid came to my door with the same demands, I would have played along and then laughed my head off. Instead a rift was formed that day. My parents tried to keep a straight face as they explained the need to respect my elders. The neighbors carried a chip on their shoulders for years. I learned early on that attitude is everything.

True, I was a precocious child, who spoke her mind, protected her loved ones and demanded justice. But really, wouldn't you laugh if a nine year old came to your home to defend her cat from your cat? My parents did use it as a teaching example, but at the same time they had already come to accept me for who I was. They never crushed me; instead they attempted to gently guide my unique energy.

I had seen the stark contrast of a good attitude toward youthfulness many years earlier when I had asked the lady in the hospital waiting room if the candy she was offering us was poisoned. She could have become a memory that stung had she been insulted by my honest question. Instead, my memory of her is sweet because she laughed as she reassured us that the candy indeed was not poison. What makes the memory even sweeter is that she brought laughter to my sick mom when she shared the story with her.

I learned that we can choose our attitudes. We can choose to be the neighbors who get angry and carry resentment with them. Or, we can be the lady in the hospital waiting room, who takes no personal offense when asked if she was attempting to poison small children. Opportunity is always hidden in the folds of struggle. We have the opportunity to change, grow and refocus; or we have a chance to wallow and blame others for our situation. The great thing is that we can chose how we respond. We can make a bitter memory sweet with the choices we make.

I had an active imagination. One of my favorite activities as a child was playing dress up. It didn't matter to me whether it was me who did the dressing up or if I was dressing up Puffy, Smokey or Tora. I loved getting lost in the imaginary world of make believe, but I was never so lost that I didn't know my way out. I also thought adults were either stupid or condescending; I wasn't sure which, but I didn't like either option.

As I played dress up with Puffy, I would often walk through base pushing Puffy in a baby carriage dressed in her Sunday-best.

Many adults would stop to talk to me.

In a cutesy little voice they would ask, "Is that your baby?"

I would answer, "No, it's my cat!"

Sometimes I was sarcastic and would answer, "No, it's my monkey!"

I would shake my head in a combination of disbelief and annoyance. Surely they were not blind to the fact that I was pushing a cat dressed up as a baby in a carriage! Puffy, Smokey and Tora all had infinite patience with me. They allowed me to dress them in ridiculous outfits and parade them around town. I, on the other hand, had zero patience for adults who couldn't clearly see the cat or dog face peering out from the human clothes.

My family always ate dinner together; however at lunchtime, I was often on my own. My dad had an aversion to cat and dog germs. I did not understand it at all. The pets were not allowed at the dinner table while we ate. I found that rule a bit rude and separatist. So, when my parents were away from the house, I would set the dinner table for lunch with a setting for Puffy, Smokey and Tora. We had four chairs at the dinner table, and it worked out perfectly. I sat at my chair with human food, and sat Tora at his assigned chair with dog food. Puffy and Smokey each sat at their own chairs with cat food. They never got up on the table to eat; they were not savages after all. We sat at our respective chairs having a civilized meal regularly.

Tora's Tricks
Tora only knew two tricks: sit and shake. That was it. Somehow we had forgotten to teach him tricks. I am sure he was smart enough. People were always showing off the tricks their dogs knew. So my brother started telling people Tora was a *dog impersonator*. He could imitate *Lassie*, *Rin Tin Tin* and *Benji*.

He would get Tora all excited and then say, "Ok play *Lassie!*"

Whatever Tora did was the right answer.

Kevin would lavish praises on Tora and tell him, "Play *Benji!*"

Again, whatever excited movements, tail wiggles and panting Tora did was the right answer. The neighborhood kids were in awe of Tora's dog imitations. I remember shaking my head and wondering what else we could trick others into believing.

Tora may not have known real tricks, but he knew true loyalty by instinct. He was game for most activities if it involved being with the family. We loved to go to Schliersee, Germany, where the Sommerrodelbahn Schliersbergalm toboggan was open all summer. We could ride the Bergbahn cable car up the mountain and ride the toboggan run back down. The toboggan was a giant mountain slide, and it was capable of reaching great speeds. It was a winding ride spanning more than one-thousand yards through sixty-three curves into the valley.

My dad had ridden down the slide with Tora in his lap countless times without episode. They were experienced and calm toboggan riders until suddenly Tora wasn't calm. There was no way out of the slide once you started, and a wreck simply meant you had to get your bearings and right yourself as you sped through the tube. For a single rider that can be easy enough, but with Tora in his lap my dad literally left some skin on the slide to safely guide Tora to the bottom. The accident didn't detour either of them from riding toboggans, sleds and slides together.

Tora wasn't deterred from much. He was such a curious dog. In Texas, he was tortured as armadillos would run surprisingly fast into holes and ignore him when he chased them hoping to play. In Germany, he chased hedge hogs, swans and geese. This time, the animals seemed to fight back. He wasn't being vicious, he simply wanted to play. Hedge hogs play dead like armadillos but they could hurt his nose with their spiky quills. Geese and swans are not even intimidated by medium sized dogs running at them; so they would run head on straight at Tora. He never learned.

Mom's Humor and Hospitality

My mom had an insatiable sense of humor. She loved to pull pranks on our friends. Our house had a revolving door of friends who made our home their second home. As we grew older, my parents allowed us each to each bring a friend with us on trips too. They did this partly because of my mom's social nature and because they understood the emphasis kids place friendships over family at different ages. The side benefits of having so many kids coming and going through our home was that my mom had even more people to pull pranks on.

My mom would excitedly ask, "Would you like to see the stars through a homemade telescope?"

All the kids would answer affirmatively. My mom would bring her victim to the kitchen window above the sink. She then placed a rain jacket over their head. She would have her victim peer through the sleeve of the jacket towards the sky. Once her victim was deeply focused on looking for stars through the sleeve, she poured a glass of water down the sleeve hitting them smack dab in the face.

The funniest part of it all was they always fell for the next prank she pulled on them. Kevin and I were willing accomplices in her pranks. We had many battles to see who could lap up spilled water with a spoon against my mom. My mom and her opponent would sit on the ground facing each other with their legs spread out. Each was armed with a spoon. My mom would then excitedly try to lap up water my brother and I had spilled on the ground between their legs. Once her opponent was lost in the competition, my brother and I would grab their legs and drag them across the water puddle. We would all excitedly declare her opponent victorious.

Even after falling for those pranks, when my mom invited them to a new game, they would play along. I think her very favorite was pretending to be able to hypnotize them. We needed four bowls of water for this game. All four bowls were exactly alike, except for one major exception. The person being pranked had black soot on the bottom of their bowl. My mom then led us all by telling each of us to dip our finger into the water and then rub along the bottom of the bowl. She instructed us to bring our finger to our face and rub it in a specific pattern. My mom was convincing.

The person being pranked would look expectedly into everyone's face. In the end, our faces were clean, but their faces were smudged with black pattern my mom had led them into making unwittingly on their own faces. My mom never tired of playing games. Decades later on her final family vacation, she played every trick she could think of on her grandchildren.

Confronting Death

Life wasn't always fun and games, though. I remember the day I was standing at the local gathering place when I heard my mom calling me home at an unusual hour. Heading towards her, I saw something I didn't recognize in her countenance. Apprehension engulfed me.

Her words tumbled out, "Robin is dead."

It was there in my front yard where I was first introduced to death. It greeted me awkwardly as I stumbled behind mom and towards our first meeting just three doors down from Robin's house.

It had been an ordinary day at the gathering place—the place where all the kids on base belonged. There were no outsiders within military housing neighborhood known as Perlacher Forst. (German for forest). Once transferred to the base, you automatically belonged to our not-so-secret society where the password to join was always, "Hello, I just moved here from . . ."

I knew nothing about death before my mom broke the news to me. Although she had died, Robin was still the vibrant girl who walked in front of me to school. She was still the high school student who was my fifth grade teacher's assistant. She was still my neighbor, and I was still working on the picture she asked me to draw.

Robin and a group of high school students had been hit by a drunk driver as they crossed the street on the McGraw Kaserne base. They were on their way to volleyball practice. My brother had been bicycling with friends to the commissary that day. He happened to see the horrendous accident and went looking for Robin's brother. Robin's twin sister and another student suffered brain damage, but Robin was already gone.

Robin's death wandered in and out of my reality until a few days later when I found myself sitting in a pew at her funeral. My bottom lip quivering, I did not know how to express my grief. Death would become an all too familiar acquaintance after Robin. As I learned through loss, only God knows the number of our days.

My Run-In With Bees

After Robin's funeral, life went back to normal for most of us. My other next door neighbor continued tanning herself until she looked like a wrinkly old raisin. The neighborhood kids went back to playing games. And I returned to chasing my brother for any reason I could find.

One time as I was running through the woods with a friend chasing my brother, a swarm of bees converged on my head. As I spun in an attempt to escape the swarm, the bees got caught up in my hair. My face, neck and head felt like they were on fire as multiple bees stung me. In my frenzied dance with the bees, my glasses flew off of my face and into the grass. The whole thing ended as quickly as it began. The bees had done their job, and I stood stunned and blind in the grassy field.

My brother quickly escorted my friend and me to the nearby emergency room. My friend was hysterical, screaming in pain and traumatized from the experience. Everything from my shoulders up was hot and stinging, but I remained oddly calm. I kept asking my brother to go out into the field and find my glasses. As the doctors pulled stingers from my head, face and neck, I lost track of their sting count somewhere around forty-seven. My friend sobbed and I thought the bees must have gotten her much worse than me.

I just kept asking the emergency room doctors, nurses and my brother to go find my glasses. I couldn't see, which was disorienting to me. All I could think of was that someone was going to step on my glasses and destroy them. Everyone kept telling me they were going to wait until evening when the bees would be in their hive. We assumed one of us stepped on their hive or knocked into it, which set the bees on a mission to protect their hive. My friend, it turns out, only had one bee sting on her side. I had received the brunt of the bees' rage. My brother had been ahead of me and he escaped without any stings at all.

My friend only had her bee sting to focus on and it caused her to freak out. I, on the other hand, was focused on my goal of having my glasses retrieved. The pain of the attack was not my focus. The doctors pulling stingers and treating multiple stings was simply an inconvenience stopping me from retrieving my glasses. I had one goal and one goal only in mind. My focus helped me not to notice the severity of the pain I was in.

For days my dad nursed my stings with chamomile tea bags and Vitamin E oil. Puffy was distraught. She attempted to nurse me back to health by licking my wounds. Eventually we had to put her in a cage beside my bed because she was unable to sleep at night without attempting to care for me. Her caring hurt in this case. I healed from the bee stings. Puffy was finally able to rejoin me at bedtime until an art project gone-wrong caused another separation.

Art, crafts and natural medicine have always played a large role in my life. I grew up in the art rooms of my mom and her artist friends. Experimenting was the name of the game; some of my favorite toys as a child were my chemistry set and my perfume kit. Growing up, we were always making one thing or another around our house.

One year we decided to take up candle making. Re-used and recycled materials were always our first choice, because our family was *eco-friendly* before it was cool. My mom and I saved up used stubs of candles with great plans to melt them all down and make one new big candle. Our plan was set in motion once we had a good sized collection.

We decided to melt our candles down in a used coffee can. My mom did all the additions and stirring to play it safe. The melting point of candle wax was higher than we expected and it took a bit to get the candle stick nubs melting. I stood by excited to make our first candle. Finally, the little bits melted down and my mom added the remains of a large pillar candle.

It turned out the pillar nub was just slightly too large for the coffee can and the pillar got stuck. My mom carefully and patiently pushed the pillar down into the melted wax below. The hot sides of the coffee can suddenly melted the pillar and it splashed down into the now boiling wax below. My height put me at the perfect level for the resulting splash of melted wax to land on my face.

Needless to say, the candle never got made. We rushed to the emergency room instead to have my burns checked out. I don't really remember much about the emergency room trip, but what I do remember is the ritual of my dad faithfully breaking vitamin E capsules and applying them to my burns night after night. Even when the actual wounds were healed and only scars remained he continued his treatments. The ritual included placing cooled chamomile tea bags onto all of my burns and then applying vitamin E faithfully, maybe it was months, but it seemed like years.

Years later, only faint scars were visible and the seeds of natural medicine were firmly planted in my mind. Today there are no scars, but my dad's use of natural cures taught me the intrinsic value of looking to nature first. Puffy had to again spend weeks locked in a cage beside my bed because she could not resist the urge to lick the vitamin E oil off my injured face.

Puffy was a wild cat at heart and the thought of her being locked up was unthinkable. Our family often traveled and left the animals to be cared for by neighbors. We wanted to lock them into the back of the house where they would get plenty of sunlight, as well as have their sandbox and food handy. It was just easier for our pet sitters to find them all. But Puffy would have nothing of it. Our pet sitters often complained the animals were never locked up when they came to check on them. Later we discovered Puffy had figured out how to open the doors and was leading the escape.

The Swedish Police Incident

One of our trips out of town was to Sweden. This became the site of the infamous Swedish police incident of 1978. We were camping along a beautiful river in Sweden. We decided it would be fun to go fishing for our dinner. My mom, not being a water person, decided not to come with us. My dad, brother and I rented a boat and all the necessities from the camp store and headed out for a day of fishing.

Somehow, and this is where the story gets murky. My mom said she heard that we would return by two in the afternoon. My dad believes he said we would be back whenever we were back. The fish were biting that day and we were determined to catch as many fish as possible. We actually caught so many fish that we had to go ashore along the way to dig up more worms.

It was by far the best day of fishing that we had ever had. We were returning victorious down the river back towards our campsite. We were floating with excitement to show Mom our day's catch as a Swedish police boat came into view.

My dad laughed and said "Wouldn't it be funny if Mom thought we were in trouble and sent the Swedish police to look for us!"

As the boat approached, we found out that was in fact what had happened. In my mom's defense, the camp store stirred the pot of her worry when they mentioned if we had gone the wrong way down the river we could have gone over the dam and perished. They failed to mention that we too had been informed of the perils of going down the river and had headed up river instead.

Mom was sure we were late. She assumed we had gone over the dam to our certain deaths. In her state of panic, she had the Swedish police called in to form a search party. The entire campsite had gotten in on the action. The other campers were standing on the dock searching the waters for signs of our boat.

The smiles were wiped from our faces as we were scolded by the Swedish police for causing my mom so much worry and for not wearing life vests. As we rowed our boat toward the dock being escorted by the Swedish police, the mob of angry campers came into view.

My brother commented, "I guess Mom won't be happy about the fish we caught!"

Mom, furious, stormed away from the dock not finding it amusing at all as we meekly climbed out of our boat with our massive catch.

Back at the campsite, we cleaned our fish in complete silence. I think we could have cooked the fish on the heat of the angry glares coming to us from the other campers. We ate in silence, still wondering how the information got mixed up so badly that my poor mom had been convinced we had died along the river, when we were having the time of our lives. Later that evening as my dad passed through camp, a young family pulled him aside to ask if he had heard about the American family who had drowned in the river that day.

Crossing Borders, Exploring New Territory

Growing up, my family camped a lot—I mean really a lot, as it was our means of seeing the world on a budget. Back then, there was a book called *Europe on 10 Dollars a Day*. My parents took this advice literally. We camped so much that as an adult I've never pitched a tent. I believe sometimes camping skips a generation. Tease me all you want, but if I never hear the sound of a tent zipper again in my life, I would die happy.

In sixth grade I got to spend a week living in a castle. My class went to Schuleinheim, which was sort of like school camp, only in a castle. I had a grand time, but I missed Puffy dearly. Our parents were given one day to come out to visit us at Schuleinheim. I was looking forward to seeing my parents, but was ecstatic when they arrived with Puffy in tow.

My classmates already considered me the crazy cat girl, so they didn't even bat an eye at the sight of Puffy. The Germans are dog people and found the arrival of a cat at their castle a bit offensive. Of everything I remember about Schuleinheim, it all pales in comparison to the moment I realized my parents really understood me. Puffy had been complaining and lonely around the house and they knew I had to be suffering in the same way. They didn't worry about our quirky connection; they fed it.

With all of our travels, I learned to love borders, borders of states, countries, time and imaginary lines that serve as worldwide dividers like the equator. I have stood with one foot in Italy and the other in the Vatican; I've had one foot in Ireland, the other in Northern Ireland. My family has driven miles out of our way to cross the Arctic Circle in Finland, the Continental Divide in Colorado and other borders around the continents.

With each crossing, I imagined all that separates the two sides. Sometimes the things dividing one side from the other seem so small and insignificant that it is hard to determine the differences. And other times the border divides economics, language, politics, religion, culture and history. Today I still hold my breath when I cross a border.

Every border I crossed as a child was different. Some border guards waved us past without checking our passports, while others like Check Point Charlie in Eastern Berlin, had more stringent protocols. The border between East Berlin and West Berlin was the most monumental one I ever crossed. I saw the evidence of those who lost their lives reaching for freedom. I never took my freedom for granted after my fingers touched the bullet holes left behind by the historical struggle of people had once been free, suddenly being walled into their city; divided and separated from their own country. When those walls fell many years later, I could hear the collective cry of freedom thousands of miles away.

As a child, I wondered if I was the same on both sides of a border. Or perhaps, I thought, I would mysteriously change as I went over the border to blend into the culture I had crossed into.

My dad always said, "When in Rome, do as the Romans do."

That philosophy must explain why my family picked up new traditions as we traveled around the globe. Eventually I realized that nothing about me changed crossing borders; I simply grew stronger as a person as a result of knowing a little about another country, city or culture. I took pieces of memory to store in the scrapbook of my mind so I could eventually relate to anyone, anywhere.

My dad's belief that we adapt to the customs around us led us into rising above many uncomfortable moments. The first time we discovered that the Germans were just as comfortable in their clothes as they were out of them was one of these memorable uncomfortable incidents. We had been excited to go swimming in our first mountain lake. We traveled up the mountain with our swimsuits packed for the occasion. We arrived in the parking lot and looked for the dressing room. Oddly, we discovered there wasn't a dressing room or a restroom anywhere in site. We looked around and saw people standing beside their cars changing clothes. They were not attempting to hide their nakedness. They were changing clothes in the parking lot as casually as one might change in the privacy of their bedroom. Culture shock never deterred my dad from any of his plans.

He announced, "When in Germany, do as the Germans do."

It turned out that changing clothes in the parking lot was the least of our shocks that day. The mountain lake was stunningly cold. We jumped in, jumped out, and ran with blue lips back to our car.

During our travels, we climbed everything. My dad has an extreme fear of heights. Despite his intense fear, he climbed beside us to great heights. We climbed mountains, steeples and bell towers all over Europe. We climbed the leaning tower of Pisa, and just about every tall building with staircases to a view point that we came across. His fear gripped him as he sometimes had to crawl the final steps of his journey. His voice quivered as he called my brother and me back from the edge. But, he never made us step fully away from the edge, just far enough back to be in the safety zone.

I remember standing on a tiny ledge with a railing was only as high as my knee tops to get a better view of the art work in a the Duomo in Florence, Italy. My Dad had plastered his body against the wall and was moving inch by inch around the ceiling ledge with us. He was consumed with fear; and yet, he refused to miss the opportunity. His discomfort was evident to everyone around him, but he shamelessly carried on.

My dad sought out these adventures for us. He loved the view, he loved the exercise and the experience, but his brain screamed out every time in protest. I would say his reaction to heights was as intense as anyone with an extreme phobia. And yet, he has never stood at the bottom of the steps or the base of a mountain. He has never allowed the fear that confronted him to make him back down from any height.

I think it was my dad's example of repeatedly facing fear and walking right into them on purpose taught me to face my fears. He never stood on the sidelines and told me how to conquer fear. He lived it by example. He did not set out to teach me how to fight fear. He simply fought his fears regularly right in front of us. He has never been ashamed of his fear, which taught me to have no shame for mine.

Emblazed in my memory is an image of my dad crawling across a mountain ridge of shale rock on his hands and knees. He looked directly at his hands in front of him, his terror leaking out of him in groans. It was a long ridge and he never once turned back, never slowed down and never gave up. I want to be an example of facing fear—whether it is on my feet or on my knees. As my dad fought his battles before the young eyes of his daughter, he showed me how a hero lives day in and day out.

While I was adventurous, nothing about me was ever graceful. There was a metal sign in the grass just to the left of the path from my home in Perlacher Forst to Munich America Elementary School, where I went to school every day. It was a road sign, which gave instruction to the drivers on the road, but was sort of in the way for the walkers. Where we walked wasn't an official sidewalk, but so many feet had walked there, that a permanent dirt path through the grass had been created. *So now can you picture it—a small dirt path through the grass beside the road with a metal sign signaling the drivers?*

The sign meant nothing to the walkers but was significant to the drivers. To this day I couldn't tell you what the sign said, but I can describe in great detail how it felt when the sharp metal of the sign grazed the left side of my head. I can tell you how it felt when my head smashed against it, nicked it and the feeling of the swish of just my hair sweeping across it. I can even tell you how it felt to hit the sign three times in a row with different parts of my head.

Why, you might wonder, would I run into the same sign time and time again? In my defense, I had a perception problem in my left eye and the sign was on my left side. I only hit the sign when I was walking toward school and I never hit it on my way home. Early on I should have found some other indicator to warn me about the sign was ahead.

It wasn't until the time I hit my head so hard that I fell to the ground from the impact that my relationship with the sign changed forever. On this particular occasion, I was disoriented and laughing so hard that when I stood up, I walked right back into the sign. I was then so stunned from the second hit that I stood up directly under the sign and hit my head again. I then crawled away from the sign while rubbing my head, no longer laughing and got up several feet away from the sign.

That day of repetitive hitting my head changed my perception of the sign forever. Before it was just a nuisance which smarted a little bit; now the sign was attacking me. In my mind, it was as if I was living in a cartoon, and the sign was chasing me and bonking me on the head.

From that day forward, I deviated off the worn path and walked beside the path in the grass for the entire length of the block. I had determined that I didn't have to walk on the dirt path. No regulation existed that said I couldn't walk on the grass. After all, the worn path had once been grass. Masses of people had walked through the grass over the same path until the grass was worn away. The original forgers of the path had made it far too close to that metal sign for my liking. I decided I could make my own path to school. It was right next to the one everyone else took but my new path was more successful for me. I could still be friends with everyone else who was on the path.

I learned to give myself permission to forge my own path. It didn't have to deviate greatly from the one I was on. I leaned that if you change your path by just one degree, it will completely change what is in your path and where you end up. If you changed your course in life by one degree, imagine what you could accomplish! In fact, if you were literally walking and you changed your direction by one degree, then each mile you would have deviated ninety-two feet from the original path. A minor change often the span of year could literally change the course and trajectory of your life.

A calculated decision to turn up the intensity of your life could also make a huge difference. After all, two-hundred-eleven degrees Fahrenheit is just hot water, but two-hundred-twelve degrees Fahrenheit is boiling water. What a difference a degree makes! There are no signs around us saying we have stay off the grass and stay on the path. Make your own path and make it decisively before you hit your head on same stumbling blocks along the path that you've been hitting time and time again. One degree of a calculated deviation from the path you are on can be the difference.

Two Distinct Paths

Along that path to school, I have two other distinct memories that shaped me. One is the memory of walking behind my sixth grade teacher to school. He walked like a penguin. He wore a long black coat and a black hat as he waddled in front of us to school. I told him he walked like a penguin, but never made fun of him. I respected him greatly. He was a kind and gentle man. He had been within range of the bomb at Hiroshima. He told me one day that you never know what a person has walked through in life and what burdens they carry unless you ask.

I always imagined the burden of his memories as he waddled to school in front of me. I never forgot to consider the unknown, unseen burdens of strangers and loved ones in my life after knowing him. I remember him every time I see a penguin and smile at the memory.

The other memory which shaped me on that path is not as fond, but had just as profound of an impact on me. One night as I walked home from the *Little Oktoberfest*, I followed a group of high school students who were high on drugs. They were bragging about their drug use and staggering from drinking at the *biergarten*. One of them carried a large maß, which is a large glass one liter beer mug. He stumbled, broke the maß when he fell and got back up. He was swinging the broken maß in his arm, laughing and carrying on when he accidentally swung it across the neck of one of the girls beside him. She barely noticed as blood began to spurt from her neck.

Thankfully adults were nearby and offered assistance because I was frozen in place and stunned. I don't know what happened to any of them, but I vowed on that very spot to never do drugs. I was terrified of them. I was also stunned that he could be so foolish, and that she could be so numb to not feel the gash in her neck or notice that any of it had happened. That moment changed the course of my life forever. Other course corrections occurred through the years, but none quite as dramatic as that one.

Overcoming Obstacles and Keeping Commitments

One year I decided to deviate from my regular sport of soccer to take up gymnastics. I've never been very coordinated, but that didn't stop me as a child from making an attempt at participating in many sports and activities. I spent a short season in ballet and tap, but the ballet teacher confided in my mom I would be better if I didn't run at everything as if I was playing football.

Although there was nothing graceful about my gymnastics abilities, I was not lacking in ambition. Four major factors were against me in gymnastics: first, I still had the issue with my vision and depth perception; second, as previously mentioned, I was admittedly uncoordinated; third, our gymnastic instructor was more interested in having fun than teaching technique; and fourth, our school was sadly lacking in proper equipment.

These four major factors played a large role in an incident that happened while I was competing for the very first time on the vault. Our team trained using a very old springboard to mount the vault. Because the springboard had very little spring left in it, we had to run full speed down the runway and jump with all our might onto the springboard in order to vault the horse. As far as we knew this measure of power was required for everyone using the vault, because we knew nothing different.

During our warm up at my first gymnastics meet, all of the teams were required to use their own springboards to practice. In practice I hurdled onto the springboard, leapt over the vault and successfully landed on several occasions. During the actual competition, we used the springboard provided by the school that hosted the competition.

When it was my turn to compete, my heart was racing from adrenaline. I stood at the start of the runway and ran with every ounce of my strength. I jumped with all my might onto the springboard. It was while in midair, long after I flew several feet too high over the vault, that I realized the tools we use make all the difference in the performance we get. The hosting school had a very powerful springboard and I over shot the vault in both height and distance.

As I flew through the air with astounding velocity, I grew concerned about my landing. I nearly flew over the end of the padded landing area as I landed with my hands still reaching down towards the vault I had long ago cleared. It was an awkward and potentially dangerous landing in a frog like stance. I sprung to my feet off the end of the mat and gave the most confident dismount pose imaginable.

I could see the concern written all over my mom's face as I walked back towards the starting point for my second attempt on the vault. I stood at the start of the runway with more adrenaline coursing through my body than ever before. I considered quitting gymnastics for a half of a second rather than making the second attempt. But quitting wasn't an option for me—it never has been and it still isn't.

I don't remember much from my second attempt, other than running down the runway much more cautiously. I jumped onto the springboard with a quarter of the power and successfully touched the vault as I passed over it. I don't remember whether I nailed my landing perfectly or not. Most likely I didn't, because I still had the previously mentioned issues against me.

I worked hard the entire year of gymnastics at the vault, uneven bars, balance beam and floor exercises. The next year I returned to my traditional sport of soccer. My speed, determination, power and strength were better suited for soccer. My perception issues and lack of grace still worked against me, but in this sport, I had more going for me than I had going against me. The greatest lesson I learned in gymnastics was to never quit something I had committed myself to do.

Sixth grade was not only the year I tried gymnastics, but also the year I started drinking. Beer was abundantly available on and off base. They sold cheap American beer in the vending machines that were stationed all over base. The Germans would then sell beer to anyone of any age off base, which was just a hop skip and a jump from just about anywhere my friends and I might have been. And everyone's parents had large stashes of good German beer that we could pilfer without anyone noticing. We snuck around with it, but only because we would have gotten in trouble with our parents.

When we drank the cheap American beer from the vending machines, we used to keep wintergreen Life Savers in our mouth to combat the foul, watered-down taste. Everyone enjoyed the good German beer. At first we hid away in the forest to drink our treasures, but over time we became bold and drank at the local German restaurants and pubs. Our gymnastics teacher introduced us to Apfelkorn, a German apple Schnapps. It soon became a favorite treat. Like I said, she was more interested in having fun than teaching us anything positive.

In sixth and seventh grade, we drank to be cool and part of the culture around us. Studies have shown that people who start drinking before age fifteen are four times more likely to develop alcohol dependence at some time in their lives compared with those who have their first drink at age twenty or older. Well, starting to drink at twelve and coming from a long line of alcoholics was the perfect combination for me to develop an early and serious addiction.

Staying in the Game

Despite my drinking, I did well in school and sports. Playing sports in grammar school taught me valuable lessons that I still use today. On the Munich American Military Base, we rarely had enough girls to form a girls' soccer team or a basketball league. In basketball we had enough girls to form only one team, which left us with no girl's teams to play against. So our one girl team played against the boy teams. In soccer we didn't have enough girls to form even a single team so they scattered the girls, two by two, onto the boys' teams. In both sports the girls had to be scrappy to survive.

Our girls' basketball team was pitiful in the talent department but we were mighty in attitude. I was never particularly good at basketball, but I played every game with all my heart. Our girls' team didn't stand a chance against the boys. When we faced the same team who had already crushed us game after game, we were always convinced this was the one game we would actually win. Despite our history, we always expected a victory. Believe it or not, by the end of the season, we actually did beat one team who had repeatedly defeated us. The audience and the other team might have been surprised, but we had been expecting victory all along.

In soccer I played on a boys' team. I made up for all my uncoordination and depth perception issues by playing soccer with the drive to win. I played the sweeper position because I had the endurance to run nonstop. I also had the singular focus to get the ball at all costs. The cost normally was a deposit of pain, sweat and blood that I gladly paid.

My soccer coach rarely let me off the field. I am not certain if he kept me in because he wanted me to earn my position on the team, if he wanted to wear down the girl on the team, or if he thought I was actually decent. But I do know I learned an amazing amount about perseverance, dedication, attitude, teamwork and never giving up against insane odds.

Our soccer league never cancelled a game due to weather. And my coach would not let our team wear sweatpants, no matter how cold it was outside. We played soccer games in the snow, ice, rain and sunshine. During snow games, the soccer ball and my skin would get so cold that when the ball hit my leg, it would leave a perfect red impression of the ball on my skin for the rest of the day. Occasionally we had the guts to whine when the other team played in sweat pants, but complaining got us nowhere. When we complained, we paid for them in the next practice. I could wave a bloody arm into the air asking to be removed from the game and my coach would simply wave back at me to continue on. I guess that is the reality of sports lead by military men.

I'm grateful for those lessons now. I learned that even when I am hurt, tired or cold to stay in the game. Whether I was winning or losing, I learned that I had to play the game to the end without complaining or making excuses. Sitting out on the benches wasn't an option, just as it isn't an option in life.

If you sit on the sidelines without getting into the game, you can't experience the thrill of victory. You don't have the growth opportunity if you don't pick yourself up from failure and play the next game with all anticipation of victory despite the odds. Don't sit on the sidelines or on the bleachers of life—get muddy, get sweaty and get in the game so you can celebrate your victories and learn from your failures.

Facing Fear

My family played hard and vacationed with gusto. We spent five Thanksgivings in a row in Obergurgl, Austria. Our tradition was to spend a solid week skiing in the Alps. At the end of each day, we always went sledding down the slope on the extremely steep mountainside our hotel was perched on. Once we went down, we had to crawl back up on our hands and knees to experience another exhilarating sled ride.

One year we even discovered how to cause avalanches. We stood at the top of the slope and rode the avalanche of snow down over and over again. We had great fun and put no thought to the real danger of our avalanches. The next year when we arrived in town, we learned that our ski instructor had died in an avalanche. Suddenly the idea of creating even our minor avalanches didn't sound fun anymore.

It was in Obergurgl where we first learned to ski. We arrived to the small mountain town during a blizzard. There were no signs of the storm dying down and our plans were to learn how to ski. Undaunted, my brother, mom and I headed out the ski slopes for our first lesson. Because of an old sports injury, my dad could not move his knee from side to side, so he took up cross country skiing instead. The storm was blowing so hard that even though my mom, brother and I stood still during our lesson, we would actually fall over. We spent more time getting up off the ground than we actually spent skiing for the first few days.

When the storm let up enough and after a few days of lessons, our instructor decided we were ready for an actual ski slope. We had graduated the bunny slopes in the blizzard. I did not share my instructor's confidence when it came to my abilities. My mom rode up the T-bar ahead of me. At the top of the mountain, our instructor gave us last minute directions. My mom went out before me and I was supposed to follow. I wanted to see what she did first and watched until she came to a complete stop down the hill a bit.

I cautiously started down the mountain towards my mom. All my lessons on how to stop or slow down seemed to instantly vanish from my mind. I found myself suddenly barreling out of control toward my mom.

She was frantically waving her arms yelling, "Cliff, cliff, stop before the cliff!"

I decided to go with what I knew best and fall down. My momentum propelled me forward. I tumbled past my mom toward the cliff. I was grabbing for a handhold in the soft fluffy snow and found none. When I came to a stop, my left ski dangled over the cliff while the rest of my body rested on firm ground. I pulled my leg up and scampered away from the edge. I promptly removed both skis and walked down the mountain vowing to never ski again.

I took up cross country skiing with my dad for the rest of the ski season. By the following ski season, I broke my vow of ski-less-ness and rejoined my brother on the slopes. My mom was willing to occasionally brave the snow, but we quickly surpassed her skills. She gladly dropped the sport.

My brother and I continued on for years and had more skiing adventures. We discovered the pearls of inattentive upward motion while skiing in the German Alps. We started talking as we traveled up the mountains, jumping from one lift to the next without noticing. After traveling upwards for some time, we took a moment to observe our surroundings. Suddenly we noticed we were the only ones traveling on a chair lift to the peak of the mountain.

The incline of the mountain was so steep that we could not ride safely back down on the lift. We had one—and only one—choice, and that was to get off the chair lift at the peak of the mountain. Although we were both very good skiers, we had never attempted a path this difficult. The only way down was to ski inside the small lip on the ridge at a frightening pace. The ridge was narrow and extremely steep. There would be no option but to tuck and ski straight down.

We decided to take a few moments to sit down and contemplate life. We ate our lunches, took *final* photographs (just in case) of each other, talked about what great lives we had led and worried about how our parents would handle our most certain deaths. Our lack of attention while moving in forward motion had left us no choice but to risk everything to get back to safety.

As I stood at the top of the path, my heart raced faster than I had ever felt it before. Every inch of my body was paralyzed with fear, but staying on the top of mountain overnight would have been a slower and more painful route to the inevitable.

I couldn't breathe as I transitioned my skis into position. On my left was a sheer drop thousands of feet down. On my right was the face of the mountain jutting at an eighty degree angle beside my shoulder, with my feet below a mere two feet of space from side to side. I could do nothing to slow my increasing speed. I knew I could not allow myself to fall and I could not lose control of my nerves.

Eventually, we worked up the courage to ski down the narrow path. I was so frightened that I couldn't even breathe in the cold air. The sound of the wind vanished. I could hear nothing but my heart pounding throughout my entire quivering body. The bright snow blurred into solid white as I tucked into position and pointed my skis straight down the mountain path. Even though the gulp of air I had so nervously sucked in was shallow, I didn't take another until I felt my momentum slow as I passed from the narrow passage into the wide ski path below. My brother followed safely behind me.

Sometimes I forget to look where I am going. Growth and forward momentum are great actions, but they should be done with planning and forethought.

Life is a race, but it isn't always about whether you win or not. Sometimes just being on the racecourse is exciting. Once while we were skiing in Austria, my brother and I got lost in conversation and didn't watch where we were going. Our lack of attention landed us smack dab in the middle of a preliminary Olympic race.

We had ridden several ski lifts up the Alps on the way to our favorite ski slope on the opposite side of the mountain. We chatted away as we rode up to the top of the mountain. Once we crested the top of the mountain we pointed our skis down the other side without even looking where we were heading.

As we were skiing down our beloved slope, we heard crowds, which were lined up along the slope, cheering us on. This noise seemed odd since normally there were no crowds lining the ski slope. The cheering got louder and louder and excitement was mounting. We were not certain why they were there or why they were cheering for us. But the cheering pumped us up and we gathered momentum as we showed our stuff, swishing down the mountain. Just as the excitement of the crowd was warming up our egos, a fast moving skier flew past us. The crowd roared with excitement.

We had skied directly into the middle of a race in progress. The air was alive with energy that infused us, despite the fact that we were in the wrong place at the wrong time. No one shooed us off the slope. We pretended we belonged there as one racer after another flew past us. When we hit the bottom of the slope, our hearts were racing and we were ready to do a victory dance of our own. When the excitement wore off, we noticed the ski lift back to the top of the mountain was not moving, so we ran awkwardly in our ski boots to the base of the ski lift.

A cranky old man operating the lift informed us it was closed because all the racers were already at the top. He did not speak a word of English. I spoke to him in German. The problem was we weren't in Germany. I actually wasn't sure what country we were in. We only knew we had to get back to Austria because that was where our hotel was. The man pointed to the bus stop and informed us we had only one way back to Austria. We showed him our lunch money and ski pass to make it clear that option wasn't going to work for us.

I figured we had nothing to worry about because I was going to stand there and plead my case until he turned on the ski lift—no matter how long it took. He insisted we take the bus or call our parents to come get us. With no money for a bus and no phone number for our hotel on the other side of the mountain, I held my ground. Eventually, he wore down. As we rode up the mountain, the crowd was continuing to cheer for the racers. We pretended they were cheering for our victorious ride on the deserted chair lift. Excitement is infectious. Just being in the race, no matter where you are on the path, is the greatest journey in life.

One year, on our annual ski trip to Obergurgl, there wasn't enough snow to ski. Instead, we hiked up a winding road with a sheet of ice that crossed it. A deep ravine lied on the side of the road. We crossed it and looked back for Tora, who had come with us as usual. He was sliding backwards towards the edge. His claws couldn't grip the ice. Tora desperately tried to get some traction. We called and called for him while we watched helplessly. We really thought we were about to watch out beloved dog die before our very eyes. Somehow, at the last moment, he got traction and made it across. If dogs had nine lives, Tora was spending his recklessly in snow and ice.

We traveled so often, that many times I wasn't even aware of what country we were in. One summer on our way back to Germany from Spain, we ended up in France. We were unaware that we were traveling through the country during a national holiday. Much to our surprise, everything was closed or full—even the campgrounds. We drove late into the night in search of a place to stay. Finally, because we were tired, grumpy and hungry, we pulled over to a rest stop. Camping overnight was not allowed, but fatigue had set in.

We were traveling in an old VW camper, which was equipped with a small kitchen. Once we stopped, our first priority was to eat. My mom whipped up an amazing meal. After dinner, my exhausted dad needed a few moments to himself to meditate. My mom, brother and I set up chairs in the deserted parking lot of the rest area to take a few deep breaths of the summer air.

Suddenly, the sky lit up with a meteor shower.

It was the most magnificent site we had ever witnessed in the sky. At first, we quietly observed. Then as the sky erupted with the most spectacular display of streaking lights, we excitedly called for my dad to come out to see what we were witnessing. He was so deeply relaxed inside the camper that he didn't respond. Later, when he emerged from the camper, we tried to explain what he had missed. But it was impossible to adequately describe the glory and splendor of the meteor shower.

We learned later that the meteor shower we saw was best viewed in the French region we happened to be in. It was also a once every few hundred years occurrence. We had witnessed this amazing event merely by chance. My dad was understandably exhausted, but kicked himself for missing the experience.

My dad always said, "A family that travels together, stays together." Actually, he applied that to whatever activity we happened to be doing at the moment. He is most commonly quoted as saying "a family that hikes together, stays together," "a family that eats together, stays together," "a family that walks together, stays together" and so forth. And it is true our that family has stayed together. But he did miss out on a meteor shower of a lifetime.

People can often look back and remember exactly where they were when they learned about significant news or specifics of the universal American story. I remember realizing we lived just on the outer edge of the typical American story when we were in a small town in Ireland. We had stopped at a local store. The storekeeper heard our American accents and his face dropped with sadness.

He said in the gravest of voices, "Tsk, tsk, you're American. I am so sorry for your country's great loss today."

Our minds raced and we thought, "Oh, no the President must have been assassinated!"

None of us wanted to appear ignorant so we accepted his condolences. We rushed to buy an Irish newspaper to read the news.

The headlines read, "ELVIS IS DEAD!"

And while his death was a great tragedy, it paled in comparison to what we had assumed.

Another time in France, while we were waiting for a candlelight procession conducted by a group of nuns from Ireland, they stopped and asked us where we were from in America. We told them we were from Dallas, Texas.

The nuns turned gleefully and inquired, "Who shot J.R.?"

Evidently the show *Dallas* was an international hit, even among nuns! Our trip was just after the famous cliff hanger that made television history.

As we travelled we were asked over and over again, "Ah, you are Americans, so who shot J.R.?"

Little did everyone know that we hadn't even seen that season of *Dallas*. Our only source of American television was AFN (American Forces Network), which was a year behind on *Dallas* and all American television shows. We actually learned on the trip that J.R. had been shot in the current season. They assumed that because we were Americans, we had gotten a special insider's scoop on the series. Their perception couldn't have been farther from the truth.

Obsolete Orthodontics

Being Americans, we caved to the same desire every other American had to have straight teeth. Unfortunately, no orthodontists practiced on base and the Germans were decades behind in orthodontic care. Undaunted, my mom found a German orthodontist. Saying that the Germans were archaic in their orthodontic practices is an understatement. They determined that my teeth were too big for my small mouth, and they had decided to pull four adult teeth to rectify the problem.

On the day my teeth we scheduled to be pulled, another kid from base had caught a ride with us to have his first exam. I remember it clearly because I can still see his pale face sitting terrified across from me after I had my teeth pulled. The procedure had been rushed. I was sent home with blood still dripping from my mouth. I was also gagging on blood as I changed the packing in the four gaping wounds. The poor kid sat across from me in our VW camper on the verge of fainting the entire way. I still wonder if he ever got braces or if my bloody mouth scared him away.

My orthodontist didn't wait for my gums to heal after extracting four large teeth. Within a week he had full braces on every tooth and was pulling my teeth quickly over the gap. The pain was excruciating. My mom always bought me cheesecake at the bakery next door because I couldn't chew for days.

By the time we returned to the States and I saw an American orthodontist, the damage was done. They had thinned my gums, left my gums sagging where the teeth had once been and pulled my teeth into a position that caused my jaw to crack, snap, catch and pop constantly. It took five years of orthodontic work to fix my teeth and surgery to repair my gums.

Frightening Incidents Near the Forest

I found many things to be afraid of in Germany. We lived on the edge of the American base known as Perlacher Forst, which was not far from the actual forest. My dad and Tora were out for a jog in the forest on a particularly frightening cold, dark winter's night. Deep in the forest, my dad could hear a howling animal. As he jogged further into the forest, he noticed Tora was missing.

Because he was worried that a howling creature had snatched Tora, he retraced his trail calling for Tora the entire way through the forest, over the autobahn and across a very busy street. He found Tora shaking with terror on the front porch of our house begging to get inside. Tora was so overwhelmed with fear because of the unknown, unseen howling animal that he ran back home to safety.

I remember the biggest search party ever assembled in Perlacher Forst was for a young girl, who was missing from base housing. The entire Perlacher Forst military base seemed to come to a standstill. I didn't know her because she was significantly younger than me, but I remember searching every basement, attic, stairwell and garbage dumpster in the area for the missing little girl. I don't remember how long we all looked, but it felt like an eternity as all the kids searched the darkest, scariest corners of our base. I think we all thought to look for her in the places we would be most frightened to be if we were alone.

She was eventually found, with one ponytail cut off and her body black and blue from a beating her daddy had given her. I don't know what happened to their family. They vanished into the abyss that all families who faced legal problems disappeared into. They were presumably sent somewhere back in America. When any kid was caught with drugs or had a serious legal run-in, the entire family would vanish from base almost overnight. Sending the family back to America was a safety net to remove American citizens from the harsh German prisons that bordered our base.

The base felt like the safest place on earth, with three scary exceptions: the German cemetery, the German prison and the base's Catholic priest. I learned later I was right to be afraid of the priest, who presided over the base's Catholic Church. He had always given me the willies. I had stopped trusting him when he told me cats don't go to heaven.

He invited all the young children to come by his office for extra sacraments, not only the bread, but also the wine. Free wine wasn't a lure to me because I could buy bad beer out of the vending machines, right next to the ice cream, candy and soda machines. A few cents was a small price to pay. It turned out our priest had been asking a much higher price from the children as he was stealing the innocence of many during extra confession sessions he conducted with them in his office.

He stood at the altar, proclaiming God's message. The smell of alcohol filled the altar and choked the aware as he slurred his words, forgetting entire passages and prayers. He served communion to the families whose children he molested during confession, promising the children salvation through their silence. He sent them out to recite their penance, slipping them candy and a wink as the children slid into the pews lost and confused. He provided Sunday school so the children of his congregation could come to know Jesus, their Shepherd, secretly praying that giving guidance to lost sheep would save his soul.

The children believed in his words. They held their tongues, crying alone for years. Eventually, the silence he imposed was shattered, and everyone became aware, but by then, he had slipped into Alzheimer's disease and would never face his accusers. Of the three things that scared me on Perlacher Forst, our priest was the only monster who could have reached us. The dead were dead in the cemetery, and the prisoners were under extreme security, but our priest roamed among us.

The safest place in the world to me was my mom's art room. I always felt like I could escape into her art room and find my own center again. The scent of her oil points, the brightness of her bold strokes on canvas and the memories of watching her paint all helped me gather in the edges of myself and feel sane.

One year, she painted the image of a bold vase of flowers on a giant canvas. I loved this painting. I would escape into her art room and add my own strokes to her canvas. She was painting thick stokes with a knife. She won first place in an art show in Munich with that painting. I always liked to dream that it was the depth I added that helped her win. But she had talent beyond my imagination. That painting hangs in my living room today. I can still vanish into the bold strokes and feel safe, feel sane and feel my mom.

Because my mom was an artist, she attracted the most interesting people. The women who have passed through my life as my mom's friends were warm breezes of eccentric flavors. They danced in and out of our lives with flaming laughter. The women I remember called me girlfriend and giggled long hours with my mom. My ears always stayed open and alert. We spent our days in painting rooms and kitchens eating all the sins that we were not allowed at home.

I remember my mom's friends laughing, but I know there were times in which they cried. It was the way they faced life that makes me remember their laughter. They were strong women—strong enough to be eccentric and to dance through life with my mom and me.

Chapter 7
Duncanville, Texas (1981–1984)

My thoughts about airplanes changed in junior high. I don't ever really remember being sad about a move until we left Munich, Germany. The summer before my eighth grade year, we were transferred to Duncanville, Texas. I was terribly distraught about leaving my friends behind. I cried at the airport, all the way through security and off and on during the long airplane ride to America. The animals all made a huge scene in their cages as we parted ways for the flight. That scene had been enough to make my tears flow freely.

I was curious about what was ahead, but my heart strings were still attached to the people I had just said goodbye to. Once in Texas, every time I saw a plane fly overhead I thought, "There is someone crying on that plane." I had never thought that before and I couldn't shake it. I relived the sadness of my separation from friends when I thought of someone else on the plane overhead going through sad goodbyes.

Later, with some distance from the experience, I finally realized that the chances of someone crying on the planes that flew overhead were actually not that great. Most people travel to go on vacation, for business or to visit people. In my mind, airplane travel had been become a sad event, when in reality, it rarely is for others. It was my own burden that had twisted my perspective on a fairly common enjoyable experience.

A Foreigner in My Native Country
After we moved back to America, it was, in general, very foreign to me. I had only lived in America for a small portion of my life. I did

not remember there being a wall of heat like the one that greeted us as the automatic doors of the airport slide open at the Dallas Fort Worth airport. It was odd to hear everyone speaking the same language. I think it was the commercialism that was most shocking to me. Everywhere I looked there were billboards and advertisements on TV and radio. The only commercials I was familiar with were public service announcements like the one that played every night on AFN radio, "It is 10 p.m. Central European time. Do you know where your children are?"

America seemed loud in every sense of the word to me. It was bizarre to feel like a foreigner in my own country. The unsettledness was exaggerated by my parent's difficulty finding a home to purchase for quite some time. We lived in temporary housing with our three pets while my parents searched.

Smokey never settled well when we moved. He would spend weeks wandering around the new home yowling at the top of his lungs. He acted as if he was perpetually lost every time we moved. But in our temporary housing in Texas, he was beside himself. He could not settle down at any hour of the day or night. We thought it was because he was getting old. Later we learned that the person before us had committed suicide in the house. The landlords had to repaint and re-carpet the room Smokey complained the most about before we moved in. He must have smelled death and old blood. He probably wondered why it didn't bother the rest of us.

When the school year was about to start, we still had no home. We had to move in with friends who lived in the school district we planned to attend. They were kind enough to take us in, but Puffy, Smokey and Tora could not join us. Our friends had a pet rabbit named Fred who wandered freely around the house.

For me, home was where my family and my pets were. Starting the new school year without them was tough. Puffy, Smokey and Tora had to go live in a kennel. I visited them every day. Watching their distress with being caged up was heartbreaking. I am certain the stress of those months used up life number five for

Puffy. I was ready to live in a shoebox if it meant our entire family would be together. There was plenty of turbulence ahead as I settled into America.

On the first day of school I was overwhelmed as I walked the hallways of Byrd Middle School. I had never seen a school building so large and was stunned to learn it only housed sixth, seventh and eighth graders. I was starting eighth grade. Munich American School only had a thousand students from kindergarten through twelfth grade. I was terrified on registration day and dreaded the first day of school. For the first day of school, I dressed in a blue and green shirt, because I was unable to decide what my favorite color was in this tumultuous time of my life.

I didn't receive a warm welcome. I was used to everyone being excited about having a new student at school. I went mostly unnoticed except by the popular girls who viewed me as a threat for daring to arrive into their territory. For many days I spoke to no one. By the time I got to history class toward the end of the day, I was exhausted from the effort of keeping myself together. We sat in rows of desks and I chose to sit at the back of the room. It was there that I learned the fine art of crying silently and unnoticed in a crowd. I looked down at my desk as if working on a paper and silently let the tears fall.

When people asked where I moved from, I would say, "Germany."

They would say, "Wow, you speak great English for being German."

I could understand people assuming I was German. After all, I looked German, dressed German, had just arrived from Germany and had an accent other than Texan. I still was in awe that people once thought I was Japanese when we moved from Japan.

A few weeks into school, I was dragging my saxophone home behind me feeling defeated.

I heard a girl's voice call out behind me, "Hey, new girl!"

I turned to smile and greet her, but her face told me she didn't want to be my friend. I turned back and walked on. She ran up behind me, grabbed my arm and spun me towards her.

She growled, "You better keep your hands off my boyfriend!"

I didn't even know who she was let alone who her boyfriend was.

I said, "Okay."

I walked on towards my temporary home. Day after day she stalked me while I walked home and reminded me to stay away from her boyfriend.

Eventually I learned her name and that her boyfriend was in my history class. He was one of the boys who gawked at me. I was desperately lonely and any attention was welcomed. I barely spoke to anyone for weeks. Later I learned that I intimidated everyone with my sullen expression, which was exasperated by the burning and squinting as my eyes adjusted to wearing hard contacts.

As an outsider, I watched the drama unfold around me. One day as I walked home, my stalker-friend stomped up to me declaring her boyfriend had broken up with her. She blamed me. I didn't care about their breakup, but hoped it would make her leave me alone.

The next day when her ex-boyfriend asked me to go out with him, I said yes. I hadn't really ever had a boyfriend. A boyfriend was a human being and I was willing to take what I could get. The loneliness was consuming me. I didn't know him from Adam, but he was a star athlete and being associated with him gained me instant friends. His ex-girlfriend, on the other hand, hated me with a passion. She never let me forget how she felt about me.

In reality, having a boyfriend was the last thing I needed. I was desperate to be loved, but I just ended up getting used. It didn't take long for me to realize that the boys who break up with their girlfriends and ask other girls out the very next day are always on the lookout for their next girlfriends. I quickly discovered my new boyfriend was the cheating kind and I broke up with him. I lost my innocence, but I gained ground in the friends department. It was too high a price to pay, but it wasn't until much later that I realized what I had lost. There was nothing healthy about any of my relationships as a teen and young adult. My brother tried, against my will, to protect me from boys. Because I wouldn't listen, he would take matters into his own hands. He towered over boys my age, and scared them as he told them that he would hurt them if they hurt me.

The stress of the move to Texas landed me in the hospital for several days with severe stomach pain. I was sent to a counselor to teach me how to cope. I didn't learn much, but it was a person to talk to, and that was worth something. When that counselor didn't seem to cure me of my sorrow, my parents moved me onto an ineffective priest for counseling.

Trying to Transform a Trashed House into a Home

Eventually my family found a house in Duncanville. Smokey yowled and yowled for a few weeks. Puffy found new hunting grounds in a nearby vacant lot. And Tora never cared about any of the changes. The house needed significant remodeling. The people before us had been going through a divorce and had trashed the house to spite each other. I had never known a single person who had gone through a divorce before. The scene of destruction in our new home was enough to give me a bad taste for divorce. Oddly, that same year, my new best friend was someone whose mom had divorced five times.

To fix our damaged house, my parents hired out the big work, but the smaller projects we did ourselves. To say my dad isn't handy is a vast understatement. Not only is he not handy, but he has the patience of a gnat when it comes to putting things together. My brother and I would start out a task with him, run laps around my dad and come back to find him still working on the same project—only he was much more upset.

When we needed to change all the door handles in the house, my brother and I finished every door except the one my dad had been working on. We came back to get our next task and found him cursing up a storm with the entire door handle disassembled before him. My dad's impatience with anything with the instructions, "Some assembly required" is actually how I discovered there was no Santa Claus. I could hear my dad deep into the night in the living room cursing up a storm as he tried to put together our presents that Santa later brought us.

My mom was also having a hard time adjusting to our move and it showed in the remodel. My mom reacted to feeling down by choosing ultra-green-green carpets contrasted by bright and light colors in the house. We really didn't notice how green those carpets were until we went away for a vacation. When we came back home, we were shocked by the extreme greenness of the carpets.

Our new home was made of pink brick and had two large mimosa trees in the front yard. My dad had a passionate hatred for mimosa trees. He proceeded to chop down, dig up the roots and plant two brand new baby trees in their place. When I gave directions to my house I always said, "You can't miss it. Look for the pink house on the corner with twigs planted in the front yard.

Establishing a Reputation and Getting Sick

No one in the eighth grade drank alcohol. I quickly introduced my new friends to booze. I made myself a homemade identification card that stated that I was nineteen years old. I made it look like a German identification card with everything written in German. I pretended that I barely spoke English. I only had to show it a few times before the store clerks decided they didn't mind selling beer to the German girl.

Adjusting to sports in a big school was intimidating. In Germany, I ran the four-hundred-yard dash. My competitive spirit always kicked in so no matter who I ran against, I won the race. In eighth grade I had to try out for the track team for the first time. Suddenly, my reputation as the fastest four-hundred-yard dash runner was no longer valid.

The coach had me run the distance by myself while he timed me. I had never learned to pace myself since I simply ran faster than everyone else. I was stunned when I didn't make the team. I failed when no one else was on the track with me to set the pace.

I had never failed at anything, so I was feeling pretty low. That weekend my dad invited me to run a one-mile Fun Run while he ran a 10K race.

He gently reminded me, "The family that runs together, stays together."

That weekend I ran the race and won.

When I went to school on Monday, I asked the coach if a six-minute mile was good or not. He immediately invited me to join the track team. I competed at the first track meet and won first place. I discovered, with each lap around the track, I actually gained speed. All those years I had been stopping short, a quarter of the way into my prime speed, when I ran the four-hundred-yard dash.

I raced in two track meets before spring break arrived. In the second meet, I came in second place and collapsed after the race. I had never felt more exhausted than I felt at that moment. I had used every ounce of energy to finish on the first place runner's heels.

Right after the track meet, spring break arrived. My family packed up for a drive to North Dakota and Minnesota to visit relatives. On road trips I was really good at sleeping, but on this trip, I excelled. I could barely stay awake at all. My parents dragged me through the sights as we made our way north and then I would immediately fall deeply back to sleep.

Our first stop was North Dakota, and even when we got there, I wasn't social. I slept and slept. When we got to Minnesota, my dad thought I should get back to running so I wouldn't be rusty when I got back in the middle of track season. I tried but I could barely walk around the track.

My parents grew concerned and took me to a doctor, took one look at me and ordered blood work. The doctor came back into the room shortly after, greatly concerned. He ordered new blood draw and explained that my white blood cell count was so out of control that he wanted to make sure I didn't have leukemia. *What!?* Now we were paying attention. He later returned to our room and announced I had mononucleosis. We continued our trip, but then my parents just let me sleep.

When we got home, I thought I was dying as I lay on the couch week after week with soap operas playing in the background. Puffy thought she was in heaven. Her person was available to be with her one hundred percent of every day. She kept me company. I had such a severe case of mono that I never returned to eighth grade except on the last day of school for a school program. I was thrilled to skip the end of the year.

Puffy's Nearly Fatal Prey
After I recovered, life went back to normal. One hot Texas afternoon, I came inside and found Puffy on the floor having seizures. We rushed her to the vet as fast as possible. She was in her teen years and we feared she was having a stroke or something else fatal. The vet gave her a quick exam, felt her stomach and then decided to do an X-ray of her body. I will never forget the image we saw on the X-ray when he returned. Inside her stomach was a full-sized, intact lizard. The vet determined the lizard was still alive in her stomach and emitting poisons in an attempt to escape.

Puffy had caught a pretty big lizard and hadn't bothered to kill it or chew it up. She had swallowed it alive and whole. Her rush to consume the lizard was on the verge of killing her. The vet gave her a high dose of laxatives to speed up the lizard's journey through her body so the stomach acids would quickly kill the lizard. As you can imagine the cure caused a few issues as well. Eating a live lizard whole used up life number six for Puffy.

Belonging in Band
By ninth grade I discovered that I had stumbled into being part of something great. I had taken up the saxophone in eighth-grade for the sole purpose of getting music credits to prepare my school transcripts for a well-rounded college application. I found myself in one of the best marching bands in the country, the Duncanville High

School Marching Band. As a part of the band, I gained some spectacular lessons from a great leader. I learned about attitude, momentum, hard work, team spirit and about being a part of something much bigger than myself.

In reality, I may be closer to tone deaf than a musical prodigy, so this story is truly an unlikely path for me to have ever been on in the first place. Yet I got caught up in something great and took part in an extraordinary experience of a lifetime. The path to my musical experience was bumpy. Because I had mono, I had missed months of musical training.

In Duncanville, being part of the marching band meant we started marching five days a week, eight hours a day during the month of August. Sometime in July, as I was chasing my brother through the house, I ran my foot into our antique sewing machine. As a result, I had broken most of my toes and fractured my foot. I spent August and most of September sitting on the sidelines watching band practice. If I hadn't shown up for practice, I wouldn't have been allowed to march after I got my cast off. I faithfully sat on the sidelines in temperatures hotter than one-hundred degrees and learned the program in my head.

In Texas, football and marching bands are an entirely different culture than any place else in the world. Duncanville High School was an award-winning band, and it held some of the most coveted records. The band was directed by Mr. Shine, who inspired me as a teenager to want to become a leader like he was. He led us into victory by holding us to high standards. He worked us incredibly hard under the merciless Texas sun, and yet, when he sent us out to do it again, we ran back out onto the field with enthusiasm.

The band was so large that we had to be broken up into multiple bands to practice during the school day. The band was divided by musical abilities. I occupied, literally, the last chair of the last band of the saxophone section. My poor placement was two-fold. Not only was I musically challenged, but I was also terrified to speak in public, let alone play my saxophone solo in public. When I had to stand in front of Mr. Shine and play, my lips and hands would shake violently, which made my playing even worse. But I was proud to occupy even the last chair in the greatest band in the State of Texas.

I've often looked back to Mr. Shine and his leadership qualities and wondered what made his students so loyal. He was a great teacher. He deeply cared that we learned from our mistakes, and he was dedicated to our education. He never asked us to work harder than he worked. He never left the field while we were out marching. Our band was huge and he often ran across the entire football field over and over again to correct and teach.

Mr. Shine was leading us to success. Even when we failed at one challenge, he put the next one out for us to reach for. If we were not champions in one event, he had us focused on becoming the champions of the next. He orchestrated the momentum of our training schedule smoothly from one competition to another.

Mr. Shine demanded a great attitude and he modeled what he wanted for us. He created a team spirit that was contagious. The team spirit was so infectious that it flowed from year to year. He wore his passion on his sleeve. He cared deeply about the success of each and every one of us just as much as he cared about the overall triumph of the band. I have no doubt in my mind that Mr. Shine loved his job.

Mr. Shine had the innate ability to relate to his entire band including, the socially awkward, the musically gifted and the tone-deaf. Our band included hundreds of teenagers who were all just as dedicated to the band and to Mr. Shine. Now that is an accomplishment.

And finally, with Mr. Shine, quitting the band was absolutely never an option—no matter how hot it was, how many times we had marched the same steps or how tired we were. We reached each daily goal before we left the field.

As part of the Duncanville Marching Band, I learned more about teamwork, victory and success than I ever did in any other sport I played. When we marched in the Parade of Champions at the completely packed Cotton Bowl, the crowd roared the moment they saw the uniform of even one of our band members. It was suddenly worth all the pain it took to get there. I was the worst saxophone player on the entire field, but my music blended in with the overall band. I was part of something remarkable, despite my weakness.

Despite my full schedule with band, my mom thought babysitting would be a good way for me to make some extra money. I had been mowing lawns and raking leaves for neighbors for as long as I could remember. My mom thought babysitting would be perfect for me. I wasn't too sure because even as a kid I wasn't very fond of kids. In my opinion kids smelled like dirt and maple syrup, and not even real maple syrup, but cheap fake maple syrup.

I took my mom up on the challenge, and booked a few babysitting jobs, which I found unbearable. Not only did the kids smell, make too much noise, misbehave and generally gross me out, but also the little boy across the street played with himself nonstop. I quickly retired as a babysitter. I resolved not only did I not want to babysit, but I never wanted to have kids of my own.

I did get a different job, which was another reason my parents decided to let me get a hardship license to drive. I also qualified for this privilege of driving at fifteen in Texas because in addition to a part-time job, I ran track before school and had marching band practice every evening.

My first job was at an ice cream shop where I made a whopping $3.25 an hour plus one scoop of ice cream per shift. I then moved up in the fast food chain and started working at a fast food restaurant taking orders for the drive-thru for $3.75 an hour. A few weeks later, I suddenly called my manager's supervisor and told her I was going back to work at the ice cream shop. My female supervisor grew suspicious of my decision to go backwards in my fast food career. She showed up at the ice cream shop and asked why I had chosen to take a downgrade in pay.

I was evasive, but she was persistent. The manager of the fast food restaurant had always made me uncomfortable by flirting nonstop with me. During my last shift, he had cornered me in the walk-in fridge. He had no intention of letting me out unless I let him put his hands all over me. My co-worker stepped into the fridge to grab tartar sauce just in time. I walked straight out the back door without looking back. The supervisor promised to fire my manager and begged me to return.

I had never in my life felt as empowered as I did at the moment. It was a time long before there were consequences to men for sexual harassment. There wasn't even a term for it at the time. But having a woman seek me out, fire my tormentor and bring me back with a raise made me realize I had a voice. My voice felt weak, but it was a voice. My manager was fired and I did come back to work at the fast food restaurant. He drove through the drive-thru often. He threatened and harassed me over the speaker, but I still felt victorious from inside the workplace.

Getting into Trouble

Somehow with my busy school, sports and work schedule, I still found time to get into trouble. Having a car transformed my world. I went from being the new girl, to being the only driving freshman. Suddenly everyone wanted to hang out. I was invited to all the parties as long as I drove. I didn't care, I was sick of being the new lonely girl at a massive high school. The marching band with the dance team and flag corps, who all performed together, had more than five hundred members. It was nice to no longer be lost in the crowd.

I think that I may still be grounded for life for all the trouble I got into during those years. Here is a small piece of advice I learned: always, and I mean always, take a potty break before the police slap the handcuffs on you. Honestly, I've only had the pleasure of wearing handcuffs three times in my life, which I know is less than some and more than others, so I don't know if I qualify as an expert on the subject or not. But the three times I found myself handcuffed, all I could think of was how badly I needed to go pee. It distracted me from concentrating on the serious subject matter at hand.

And, a small matter of housekeeping: I only broke the law the first two times. The third time I was completely innocent. My first run-in with handcuffs includes my teenage stupidity and the long wait in the back of a police car. My friends and I were out on a dark road drinking beer when a police car pulled up on us. He busted us for underage drinking.

He slowly poured out our beers, one by one. That night I performed the longest stationary potty dance ever waltzed. The slow pouring beer was added torture. I took a somber trip home and had a forced confession to my parents once I arrived. In the morning I found out one of my friend's dad knew a judge and got the entire incident thrown out. It was too late for that particular grounding and sadly I didn't learn a lesson.

I think the first few years of driving I was more of a bumper car driver than an actual driver. I drove a giant obnoxiously bright orange Volkswagen station wagon. From any tall ride at Six Flags over Texas you could spot my car in the parking lot. It wasn't the most reliable of cars either. One time it broke down in a location where I was not supposed to be. My brother came to my rescue, and towed me home. We were not well trained, however, in the fine art of towing. We used a rope to pull my car by the bumper. Much to our surprise the bumper ripped right off my car. I watched it drag behind my brother as I sat motionless in my dead car. The ripped off bumper was even harder to explain than being in the wrong place.

On another occasion, I drove off with the backdoor still open and ripped it off. Driving was expensive for me. My parents made me pay for all my mistakes with the money I had earned working. I also drove over a train track too fast and my engine fell out onto the road. You try explaining why you were five miles from church when you were supposed to be at youth group. Lying was an art form I had mastered.

Between my stupid decisions and foolish lying, I was grounded a lot. And I mean a lot. Puffy loved the extra time with me. I wasn't allowed to talk on the phone either, so I comforted myself with long talks with Puffy. The only time I was allowed to leave home was for work, school, sports or my volunteer job as a Candy Stripper at a local hospital. I couldn't quit anything other than my volunteer position. I got the bright idea to quit there and not tell my parents. Needless to say I got caught in that lie too.

During my ninth and tenth grade year I dated a boy in the drum corps of the marching band. In marching band world, the drum corps guys are like dating the quarterback of the football team. Our football team was so terrible at the time the marching band people were just as popular. I found myself adjusting to life in Duncanville just in time for my dad to be transferred.

Chapter 8
San Antonio, Texas (1984–1986)

I entered two of the hardest years of my life abruptly. Those years I refer to as *the years I don't speak of*. After three years in Duncanville, we packed our bags for our transfer to San Antonio before my junior year in high school. This was the first move I made without my brother by my side. He had graduated high school and had headed to college.

I had only lived in San Antonio a week when I unexpectedly discovered I wasn't welcome there. I was in a rough school district with a mostly Hispanic population. The other high school girls were not excited about the arrival of a new blonde chick. I had barely recovered from the move when my initiation into my new reality began.

I realized my arrival to San Antonio wasn't going to be smooth on my first and last day at a new job at a BBQ restaurant. The hours couldn't pass fast enough. The girls who worked with me hated me simply for being another female. They physically threatened me. I decided a minimum wage job wasn't worth a return visit. I don't even think I told anyone I wasn't ever coming back. I just left my uniform there and walked away.

I was shaken from the experience. I sat in the parking lot trying to gain my composure. It was there that I realized that I couldn't remember how to get home, my address or what my phone number was. I inched my way out into the street and headed in the direction I thought might have been the way I had come. My orange Volkswagen had died, and I was driving a new light blue Datsun.

As I traveled down the road looking for familiar landmarks, I fell apart. I started to cry uncontrollably. I was lost, profoundly lost. I had no idea how to find my way home. Just then I saw the flashing lights of a police car in my rear view mirror. I was certain he was coming to my rescue. He found me sobbing in the front seat of my Datsun. Much to my surprise, he ignored my tears. He sternly informed me I had been speeding.

I explained that I had just moved to San Antonio and was completely lost. He asked me where I lived. He was not humored by the fact that I had no idea. He took my license and went back to his car. He returned with a ticket for speeding and a warning that I had only thirty days to change my address on my license. He actually drove away. He left me sobbing in my car on the side of the round, and I was still quite literally lost.

During *the years I don't speak of* it felt like I was living in a dreamworld. Nothing made sense when compared to the reality of my past. Before that day, I would have expected the police officer to help me. But somehow, I was living in a different world, which was so unfamiliar and disorienting.

That day I drove for what seemed like an eternity until I stumbled upon streets which started to look familiar. I finally found my home and wept inconsolably. My parents tried to comfort me. They said it was only a speeding ticket, but it wasn't the ticket at all that I was upset about. It was the paradigm shift. In reality it was the first tremor in what would become an earthquake-like period in my life. My constant companion, Puffy, tried to lick away my tears, but even her comfort couldn't ease the pain.

Nothing in my life seemed familiar, even the constants like my family and Puffy. The changes threw me off-kilter. It created a struggle in me to find a new reality. I was humbled by San Antonio and the two years I spent there. I found a new job at Albertson's not far from my high school. It was there I had a uniform to wear and accented it with my bright blue boots. I was a nonconformist even when in uniform. One of the guys who worked with me nicknamed me Blue. I had always resisted nicknames.

When people called me by anything but Kayla I would say, "Just call me Kayla."

But this time I allowed it. The nickname "Blue" fit me in more ways than one. I wore blue on the outside, but I was deeply blue and sad on the inside. Blue became my favorite color again because it defined me inside and out.

I arrived at my new—and what would be my last—high school travel-weary. The move to San Antonio was simply one move too many in my teenaged opinion. I certainly let my parents know I was not a willing participant in this move. I had dragged my feet, wailed, cried and eventually reluctantly left behind my friends and boyfriend. It didn't mean that I was prepared to make new friends all over again.

In the middle of the school year, my mom asked me to do her a favor. She had a friend who needed someone to drive her Chilean foreign exchange student to school. Her friend lived between our house and the school. The foreign exchange student felt he now had his own personal driver, who had been hired to not only transport him, but also put up with incessant flirting and ogling mixed with a masculine sense of superiority over me.

I drove him in silence, brushing off his constant come-ons as cultural. He hated that he couldn't upset me and get under my skin. One day, while I drove down a busy four lane road, he reached over and pulled up the emergency brake of my car. The car spun in circles in the middle of the road as I fought for control of the steering wheel. He held up the emergency brake so I couldn't take control of the brake.

We sat stranded across two lanes of traffic going in opposite directions.

I glared at him and yelled, "What did you do that for?"

He howled in delight with having gotten a reaction out of me and laughed, "Because I wanted to."

I drove him the rest of the way home, silently seething at him. I didn't want to feed his all-consuming ego. I dropped him off and reported the incident to my mom. She took care of the rest. I never drove the Chilean foreign exchange student again.

My parents owned my car, but I was in charge of paying for maintenance and gas. I liked the responsibility of being in charge of my car. I kept it clean and maintained it regularly. I was thrilled when I got all brand new tires. I filled up the tank with gas and was ready to go show off my new tires to my parents.

We lived off of a large road called NW Military Highway. It was an extremely busy road. I waited patiently at the exit of the tire store with my brand new tires waiting to pull out and test their grip on the road. Absentmindedly, I reached over and pulled on my seatbelt. It was long before seatbelt laws, but my dad always insisted we wear them. I always wore my seatbelt around my dad, but I didn't wear it my myself. I must have subconsciously been thinking he'd be waiting outside for me to pull up and show him my tires.

I pulled out onto NW Military Highway and brought the car up to speed. Just as my speedometer read fifty-five miles per hour the truck beside me sped up and did a sudden U-turn in front of me. In slow motion, my car T-boned his truck before I could even put on my brakes. I hit him full force at fifty-five miles per hour. I braced as we hit only to find the seatbelt holding me into my seat. As metal crunched, I watched my hood crinkle like paper onto my windshield.

Just moments after the accident, my brother passed by. He didn't even recognize the wreckage of my car. He must have been coming for dinner from his college dorm at Trinity University. He got to the house and reported that he had passed a really bad accident on NW Military Highway.

With adrenaline flowing after the impact, I jumped out of my car to check on the other driver. He drove a large Texas-style truck. It was totaled, but it fared better than my little Datsun. We walked over to the nearest apartment building to borrow someone's home phone. He insisted on using the phone first. He called a friend and whispered something urgently to them. I then called 911, and followed that call with a call to my parents.

As we waited by the wreck for the police, I started to wonder what he had whispered on the phone. Suddenly another car pulled up to our accident site. The driver of the truck reached behind the driver's seat and grabbed a small brown paper bag. He brought it to his friend and the other driver raced away with the brown paper bag. I realized suddenly that the driver of the truck was high. He had just had a friend take off with his stash of drugs. When the police arrived, I begged them to test the other driver, but with no obvious evidence, they refused.

My worried parents, fueled by reports of the accident from my brother, arrived on the scene. I insisted I didn't need medical attention. Once all the paperwork was handled, they drove me home. I was still in shock. It was obvious the car was beyond totaled. I kept wondering if I could keep my brand new tires. It wasn't until we got home and the shaking stopped that the pain set in. I had never suffered from back pain before that day, and I would never live a moment again without it.

Two weeks after my car accident, I started a job at a large department store. I was taking pain killers for my back and felt like I was moving at half speed, but I guess I wasn't. When I started my job in the shoe department, I was given a quick overview by that department's manager and then left on my own.

My job was to keep the shoe department clean and stocked. I discovered that I could do that in the first hour of my shift. I didn't know what to do with myself for the next four hours. Because no one was around to ask, I decided to reorganize the shoe department and stock room. Within a week, the area was transformed, and I left a note to the next shift employees to explain the new system.

During the next week, I continued to search for projects. I started cleaning up and organizing the departments that bordered my department. One day, the manager of the store came up to introduce herself to me.

She asked, "Would you like to become the supervisor?"

I replied, "I'd love to be the shoe department supervisor."

She laughed, "No, I mean would you like to be the supervisor of the entire store?"

I glanced out at the massive store and said, "Well, of course!"

I spent my junior and senior year of high school as the store supervisor on the night and weekend shifts at the department store. I can't say that all the adults who worked for me were thrilled that a seventeen-year-old shoe department clerk was suddenly their supervisor, but over time, I gained their respect. The next logical step up for me was to become the supervisor of the office department as well. I swapped back and forth filling both roles during my tenure there.

Our store was a regional training store, which meant we trained new managers for other stores in the area. We normally had at least one manager-in-training at our store at any given time. I trained them on all levels of the store management. I excelled at it, until a young manager in training started coming up behind me and grabbing me. I respectfully asked him to stop, but instead, he escalated his advances.

This time, however, I was the one entrenched in my job and unwilling to leave. I reported his behavior, and his career in management ended. But for a moment in the harassing, I went from feeling like the one in charge to being small and controlled. On the day I saw him being escorted away from my store, I felt just a little bit bigger, and just a little bit more powerful. It felt good. It would still be years until sexual harassment even had a title, but I knew I never had to stand for it.

I'm not sure why I was harassed so much as a teenager living in San Antonio. I wondered if I wore an unconscious sign that read, *"Victim."* Even though I excelled at school and work, I suffered a nonstop onslaught of unwanted attention.

I had moved enough to be a professional new kid at school. The hardest part of being new at school was always the free time in between classes and lunch period. It was the lulls between the class periods in which I perfected the art of faking it until you make it. I walked through the hallways with my head held high with great purpose in my stride.

I had learned no one ever bothered a confident new kid who seemed to have someplace important to go. At this particular high school, that important place I was going was often a bathroom stall where I could hide to erode the extra minutes between classes. But bathroom stalls were not appropriate places to hide at lunchtime. People would have wondered what I was doing if I carried my lunch tray into the girl's bathroom.

I tackled lunch period by purposefully never wavering on the direction I was heading. I never paused or asked permission to join a table. I simple strode to my chosen spot alone and sat down as if I was expecting someone to join me at any moment. I did this because I was too proud to let my loneliness show, but the end result was my apparent confidence attracted people. Kids started joining me and, over time, they became my friends. These kids never knew they had befriended a shell of the girl I had formerly been.

Sinking in Darkness
No adult could really reach me in my dark teenage brokenness, but Puffy could. She was my rock, my roots and my constant un-judging companion. I cried countless tears that she licked them away while purring softly. I am surprised she never got salt poisoning for all the tears I cried. Puffy alone could comfort me, but she couldn't talk me out of the dark hole I crawled into. I was wedged in tight, refusing to exit.

I affixed myself to the darkness daily, hiding vodka in the bottom of my laundry basket and punching walls until my hand was bloody. I beat my chest to try to make the pain on the outside counter balance the pain on the inside. I was drowning.

San Antonio seemed to me to be an impossible mountain to climb. At my school the boys jeered and leered at me. There was innuendo in their every word and glance. And they showed a total lack of restraint from reaching out and inappropriately touching me.

Because of their attention, I gained the hatred of the girls at the school. The girls carried razor blades in their cheeks and would dangle them out on their tongue to taunt and terrify me. They threatened everything from maiming to killing me.

Because of their threats, I refused to go into the locker room. I already had two years of P.E. classes, two years of track credits and two years of marching band credits, all of which more than filled the high school physical education requirement. The school didn't agree and tried to force me to take P.E. class, but I refused. My parents fought and won the battle for me.

I was so constantly afraid, desperately sad and furious with my parents for bringing me into my own personal hell-hole. I complained to them, but honestly I was so embarrassed by the way the boys treated me like a piece of trash art. I couldn't bring myself to tell them the whole story. I still had the echoes of my childhood molester echoing in my head, "It is her fault." That babysitter's lie had hardened into a trail of self-loathing causing me to resent the voices in my head.

With the stress my grades began to suffer. I had always been in the honor program at school, but never thought anything of it. Until one day my high school counselor called me into her office.

She said, "I am really disappointed in your grades so far here. I had expected more of you. If you keep it up at this rate you will not graduate at the top of your class."

And suddenly, I was listening. Because I was competitive by nature, she was speaking my language. Previously I had no idea I was even in the running for graduating at the top of my class. I fixed my academics overnight, but the rest of me was still dying a little bit each time I walked through the doors of the school.

I drank and partied mostly with older kids who were out of high school. Occasionally I mixed with some of the crowd from my high school at parties. I still had my boyfriend back in Duncanville. Being unavailable was not popular with the guys at my school. I got asked to prom over and over again. I declined all the invitations. Some of the boys felt threatened by my lack of interest in them.

Rumors spread one weekend that I had had sex with the entire football team on the hood of a truck in the parking lot of a local hang out. I had been out of town that weekend. I was surprised to hear the rumors, but I tried to hold my head high while I walked through the sneering crowded hallways. In private moments I vanished into the girl's bathroom to cry. Bullying did not have a title back then, but it was alive and well.

I was in constant trouble at home as my rebellion reared its ugly head against my parents. I was so bitter and angry. I was completely unable to see the rationale behind keeping a job that forced us to move against our will. My grief sucked me dry. I had no energy for even the people who loved me.

During one particularly heated argument with my parents, my dad yelled, "If you don't want to live here and you refuse to live by our rules, then by all means leave. You can take nothing that belongs to us."

I took this as a literal invitation to leave.

I had been earning my own money and socking away it way in a college fund for years. I had nearly ten-thousand dollars. I figured that was enough to make a new life for myself. Bitterness and anger warred for first place within me. I packed my clothes into a five gallon bucket, booked a flight to Dallas, made some phone calls and left a key to my car with a note telling my parents they could come pick it up at the San Antonio airport. I figured they would not notice I was missing until they got off home from work. By then I would be long gone. I had the short sightedness of a rebellious, hurting teenager.

As I sat at the airport casually chatting with someone beside me, I was stunned to see the faces of my very angry parents marching towards me. I had missed my escape by minutes. One of my friends who I had called in Duncanville had ratted me out. My parents told me I had two choices: go back to work with one of them or go to school. I glanced at my watch and decided it was almost time for German class, which was my one refuge at school.

My German teacher recognized my grief and kept me in her classroom with no questions asked for the entire day. I came home to find that my parents had found me a new therapist for me. This time it wasn't a priest and it wasn't a flunky counselor, but a real doctor of psychology. My parents required me to invest in my own therapy by paying twenty dollars toward each session.

For two years, I sat on a couch in counseling to work out my demons. Sadly, while my counselor was good, he could only get me to dig so deep. I never told him about being molested as a child. I never talked about my drinking. And I never ever told him what happened in San Antonio during the course of our sessions. My shame was too great. He still was able to dig me out of the sadness that had consumed me. My parents and I restored our relationship under his guidance.

Eventually, my constant rejection of the disgusting attention of the high school boys reached a fevered pitch; when I found myself drunk and pinned down under one of the athletes at a party. I screamed for help, wrestled and fought. The pounding music of the party drowned out the sound of my screams.

He kept saying, "I know you want it, I know you want it!"

Repeatedly I screamed, "NO!"

The little girl, who knew it had all been her fault at eight years old, believed it was her fault again. It was if time stood still, and in a forever second, I lost all the ground that I had gained. Some say memory blurs in crisis, but mine didn't. I remembered and relived every moment of that night for years. It replayed and haunted me.

I went home and finished off whatever vodka I had hidden in my laundry basket. I summoned up the courage to write my boyfriend a "Dear John" letter with no explanation. I sent it to him with his class ring as I shut down my emotions. I avoided his calls for days. I waited for the letter to do the speaking for me. When he got my letter, he made the five-hour drive to San Antonio. I was still ignoring his calls. He begged and pleaded for an explanation, but I had vacated my body and could give him none. Even as he sobbed, I had nothing to offer.

I just kept repeating, "I'm sorry, I'm sorry."

In my mind, I had apologized for being raped and being unfaithful. I'm sure that in his mind, I was apologizing for breaking up with no explanation.

In response to the deadness that consumed me, I immersed myself in the party scene. I surrounded myself with people who drank heavily and did drugs. I never partook in the drugs, but it was everywhere around me. I drank shots of tequila next to the guy snorting lines of cocaine. I thought nothing of it. It was the new normal. The culture was to see who could get more messed up than the other person. The emptiness was invasive. I felt emptier and emptier with each hangover I woke up with. I told myself that at least I didn't take drugs. *I wasn't that bad.*

I saw the good kids at school and I wondered what kept them that way. *What drove them to never cross the line?* I didn't wonder out of disgust. I didn't think that as a partier I was above them. I wanted to know what in life was worth staying sober for. Most of the kids who partied also went to church with me or attended the other local churches. I never imagined it was religion or faith that made them different.

In order to live my wild party life, I had to keep improving my art of lying. I lied so much to my parents that I even believed myself. I would get mad at them for accusing me of lying in the midst of a lie. I had my mind so wrapped around the justification of my lies that I had myself convinced. I think I could have passed a lie detector test. I told the lies so often that they actually started to seem true to me. I was blinded even from my own truths. In the twisted emotions of my hurt and anger, my mind rationalized everything I did even the vilest of choices.

I put my lying to the test at a Cinco de Mayo festival in downtown San Antonio. A group of us were blatantly carrying glasses of beer through the festival. A police officer carded us. I had gone downtown purposefully carrying no identification. I gave him a false name. He called it in and discovered my lie. Even after he handcuffed me, I refused to change my answer. I sat in downtown San Antonio handcuffed, defiant and cornered with my lie. I guess he decided he had bigger fish to fry because he let me go. I was on the verge of confessing in exchange for a potty break. Getting away with my deceit only built my confidence and led me further astray.

Victim of A Crime
My next encounter with a police officer was as a victim. One evening while stopping to get gas just outside my neighborhood, I came across a male friend who was being harassed for being white by two Hispanic men in their twenties. I asked my friend if I should call 911.

He said, "No."

He was trying to ignore the harassment as best he could. After he finished pumping his own gas he waited in his car to make sure they didn't turn on me after he left. As my friend and I drove off in opposite directions, I noticed the two men as they climbed into their pickup truck.

A few miles down the road, the stillness of the late night was broken by distant speeding headlights approaching in my rearview mirror. The two men approached my car, and out the open window of a Chevy truck the passenger sliced the night air with the edges of a switchblade. I increased my speed. The truck appeared beside my car and the two men laughed at my terrified face.

My hands squeezed the horn and it blew deep into the night. My speedometer read seventy-seven miles per hour and was increasing, yet his arms, the knife and their voices stayed with me. I raced down Military Highway trying to get to the heavily populated area around the grocery stores. A scream swallowed my voice and I choked as the two men passed me, crossed my path and skidded to a stop. My wheels squealed, engine died. I turned the keys, pumped the gas and found no escape.

I checked: doors locked, windows up, and horn blowing into a hot San Antonio night. One man flew out of the white truck and threw his body on my car, trying to find a path into my car, to carry out his threats. His shoulder smashed against my window. I sat immobilized by fear as the horn blew, cars passed by me, and apartment lights all around were off. I sat and rocked. I screamed and watched the glimmer of his switchblade as he carved into my windshield.

With one great effort, he threw his body against the passenger window. I heard the glass crackle against his body. He was so high that he must not have heard it. Just then, he walked back towards the truck, bouncing with glee for having terrified me. What followed was silence; he was gone. The taillights flickered; the driver put the truck into reverse and crashed into my car. My body jolted and my hands bent back against the horn. My senses returned as I watched them drive away.

My entire body was shaking, like it was in a horror film, and I fumbled to restart my engine. I raced to the local grocery store and ran to the customer service desk, screaming incoherently for help. The clerks called the police. I distinctly remember the heartbreak in my dad's voice as he tried to understand my frantic phone call. As I waited for the police, I sat on the cold floor of a grocery store, just four minutes from home, beside the bubble gum machines repeating the license plate number aloud.

By morning, my dad had already made arrangements for my damaged car to be removed from our driveway. I was silently grateful to miss seeing the damage by daylight, almost as if I could pretend it was simply a bad dream—but it wasn't. It took me at least ten years to ever pump gas at night again. Even now the combination of a hot night, the smell of gas fumes and an unknown stranger nearby can give me a moment of pause.

Puffy Ages and Loses A Friend

Thankfully between the various traumas in San Antonio, there was laughter still in our home. Puffy didn't adjust well to our move to San

Antonio either. She became naughty and liked to pee in the most unlikely places. But because she defined love for me, my parents had to tolerate her antics, no matter how bad they were. As Puffy aged, she found some of the strangest places to urinate. She drowned my cactus, put out the pilot light on the stovetop, and turned a favorite houseplant yellow. She used anything that appeared to be a proper receptacle to her. One week, we all sniffed our way around the kitchen attempting to find the source of the odor that gave away her secret. Days passed as we hunted unsuccessfully.

Finally, when my mom went to add more fruit to the fruit bowl on the kitchen counter, she found the fruit resting in a puddle of cat urine. Puzzled, she asked my dad how he hadn't noticed the liquid in the fruit bowl. After all, he ate fruit from it every day.

He replied, "Of course I noticed the banana juice."

Thank God he was in the habit of washing his fruits before eating them! My mom and I howled with laughter. My dad, already not a cat fan, still to this day does not think it was funny. In fact, I wanted to submit this story to Readers Digest, and my dad would not give his permission.

Smokey and I were the same age. We had gotten him just as we arrived in Japan. I was six months old and Smokey was a kitten.

When Smokey and I were eighteen years old, Smokey died. It was the first major pet tragedy in our family. We were crushed. Puffy and Tora were distraught. They both spent weeks curled up in Smokey's bed. Later, Puffy would abandon the bed, but Tora made it his own for the rest of his life. Puffy's age and sorrow seemed to combine to use up life number seven.

Dealing with Flash Floods of Grief and Water

Shortly after Smokey died, my mom and I had a communication breakdown. I didn't know what to do with my grief over losing Smokey. For my entire childhood, I had the same animals in my home. Not only was I sad for my own loss, but I had great sympathy for my mom because Smokey was her baby.

The communication breakdown occurred when I thought my mom was giving me clear instructions on how to bring a new cat into our home. My mom kept telling me how she really wanted a new kitten, but my dad wasn't sold on the idea. She told me all about the kind of kitten she thought would melt his heart and win a place in our home. I took this as a clear instruction to go find a kitten and plop him on our doorstep so he could win my dad's affection.

Now, I don't know what I was thinking. Admittedly, my brain had fallen out of my head as a teenager. Or maybe it was the shared heartache my mom had and the imbalance in our home without two cats and a dog. But I honestly thought my mom was telling me, *without telling me out loud,* to go find this perfect kitten and bring him home. Never to be one of inaction, I started visiting a lot of kittens during the next few days. When I found the perfect match, I purchased him. I came home while my parents were out and planted him in our fenced backyard. I then headed off to the movie theater.

While I was watching the movie, my dad appeared. He asked me if I left a kitten in the backyard. I didn't think it was part of my mom's plan to tell him the whole story.

I innocently asked, "What kitten?"

I came home to find my mom delighted and playing with the little grey tiger kitty that I had purchased. She had even temporarily named him Sweet William, which is exactly the name she said she was saving for the new kitten she dreamed of having. We plastered the neighborhood with signs for a "found kitten." I felt confident no one would claim him. My dad melted and agreed if no one claimed him we could keep him.

Many years later when Willie (as we called him for short) was nearly six years old the whole story came out. My parents and I were out for a walk along the Rhine wine country talking about how a cat bought from a private home was better emotionally balanced than a store bought cat.

I pondered aloud, "Maybe that is what is wrong with Willie?"

And in the silence that followed I realized my blunder.

My dad exclaimed, "I knew it!!!"

What surprised me was my mom's shock that I had purchased Willie. I explained how I was simply following what she asked of me to do.

My parents and I laughed all day about the revealing of the Willie secret. He was one of my dad's favorite cats we ever had. No wonder since I had purchased him with the specification my mom had given me to win my dad over. But she was merely daydreaming. I had taken action on her dreams. I've never regretted it and my parents had many years of joy with the antics of Sweet William. But it was a classic case of miscommunication. I assumed when I clarified what my mom's dreams were she was asking me to make them happen.

The communication breakdown between my mom and me was harmless and still makes my dad laugh till he snorts. And that alone fills me with great joy.

Not long after Smokey passed away and Willie joined our family, Tora became terminally ill. Our original furry family went from three to one during my senior year of high school. Puffy, once the middle child, became the old lady of the house. The loss of Tora was heartbreaking for the whole family. He was everyone's best friend. To Puffy, Willy the new kitten, was no substitute to her long-time companions. I worried she would be following in their footsteps as I prepared myself for college. Again sorrow seemed to absorb life number eight for Puffy. She was growing older before my eyes.

That year would bring human loss too. Late one night as I laid awake in my bed, I found myself reaching for the phone before it even rang. I knew with all certainty that the sound of the phone would pierce the darkness to inform our family that Grandpa had just passed away. With tears of loss already stinging my face, I brought the phone to my mom knowing I was handing her heartbreak on the other side of the phone. I knew I'd be answering the call from my mom's brother just shortly after the holidays.

My grandpa had spent Thanksgiving and Christmas visiting all of his family members. We played cards together as we had throughout our lives. In Bismarck, North Dakota my grandpa was famous. They even dedicated an entire day and softball complex to him. In my eyes he was perfect, despite the fact that I could not always understand his mumbled words.

I fondly remembered the time he visited us in Germany and said as we turned toward the Alps, "You can't see anything with all these mountains in the way."

I suppose North Dakota made him hungry for undisturbed spaces. I loved my grandpa unconditionally, even when he choked on his food at the dinner table. I loved his arthritic hands as they shuffled a deck of cards and sloppily dealt out our game. I loved the uneven sound of his breath escaping as he waited for me to play my hand. I had been expecting the news that Grandpa had folded his hand and left me to play solitaire all day, but I still wasn't prepared for it.

It seemed life was filled with one flash flood after another of grief in a land where real flash floods were common. The ground in San Antonio only had a thin layer of top soil above limestone. The water had no place to go in sudden rainstorms. Every low point in town was susceptible to becoming a raging river. On the road between my high school and home was one of those flood zones.

Along the side of the road was a permanent measuring pole. It was placed there to forewarn drivers about the flooded road. Most of the year, the road was completely dry. Sometimes the road was covered with low and still waters. At either of these times, drivers simply experienced a slight dip in the road when passing the measuring pole. But occasionally, cars would be washed away when they drove through without checking to see if they were passing through low or high water.

I was especially careful when I approached the area while it was raining. I wasn't afraid to turn around and go the long way home. Many drivers were willing to tempt their fates and edged their cars out into the water as they crossed the road. The water seemed harmless and looked low, but it didn't take very high water to sweep cars away. What always surprised me was how many people were willing to wander out into danger just to take the short cut. There was another way to the major road that we were all trying to get to. The other way was longer, slower and a bit out of the way, but it was guaranteed not to flood.

Only the drivers who ignored the warning signs and crossed the water got swept away. The remnants of this memory flash vividly in my mind whenever I consider the common phrase, "taking the high road."

An Unplanned Rescue

One evening my mom and I were taking the long way home from an evening movie. We were chit-chatting with each other as we drove, when suddenly several cars collided in front of us. I was far enough behind the cars and easily avoided the accident. I pulled the car over behind the accident to see if anyone needed help.

As I got out of the car, I noticed that one of the vehicles was rolling away. I sprinted to catch up to it. I ran beside the car and yelled into the open window for the driver to put her foot on the brakes. She sat limp in the driver's seat, dazed and unmoving. Her hands were not on the steering wheel, and the car was moving toward the side of the road. I repeatedly banged on the side of her car to jolt her out of her fog. But she didn't respond. Her foot was on the accelerator, and soon, she would end up going off the side of the road.

Before I could think about it, I had flung her car door open and jumped onto her lap. I put enough pressure on the brakes to counteract her foot on the gas, and I steered us to safety. Once we were out of harm's way, I pulled the emergency brake and put the car into park. I lifted her leg off the gas pedal. I had literally sat right on top of her and over-taken her car, and she still did not react. As I climbed off of her lap, the emergency responders were approaching the car.

I handed her over to the experts. My mom and I gave our statements to the police before we drove home. My adrenaline was still on overdrive, but it made me think about the fact that my plans for the evening had only been to see a movie with my mom. I had not planned in the morning to sprint down NW Military Highway and jump onto the lap of a driver in a moving vehicle. If I had planned ahead for such an activity, I would have worn better shoes.

Adventures related to vehicles were common for my mom and me. One afternoon we were deep in conversation as we pulled up to the mall and parked our car. We always parked near the same mall entrance. It offered the fastest escape route from the car, through the scorching heat and into the air-conditioned mall. As transplants, our internal thermostats couldn't adjust to the heat and humidity of San Antonio. The walk from the car to the mall entrance was always briefest when we parked near the East mall entrance; it was a family favorite.

My mom and I continued our dialogue as we shopped. We were there for a purpose, and once we completed our purchase, we were ready to escape the crowds and head home. My mom and I had a comfortable relationship by this time. We could easily get lost in conversation. We navigated our way home with the car filled with laughter and the chatter of mother and daughter.

It wasn't until we had been home for quite a while that we discovered something about our outing wasn't quite right. My dad and brother then came home all worked up. They too had gone to the mall to do some shopping. We hadn't seen them there. When they finished their shopping trip and went out to the parking lot, they found their car wasn't there.

They had gone to the exact parking spot where they had left their car—and it was gone! The incident was long before cell phones and cars that beeped at you when you pushed a button on a remote key fob. They searched and searched for their car under the hot San Antonio sun. It was nowhere to be found. They were beginning to believe their car had been stolen when they stumbled upon my mom's car sitting in the same parking lot.

They realized what had happened. My mom and I had gone to the mall in her car and we left in my dad's car. We hadn't even realized the difference. We had all parked in the same parking lot, but since my mom and I were lost in our banter, we didn't even think twice when we walked up to my dad's car and drove it home. When my brother and dad arrived at the mall they had found a better parking space closer to the entrance then we had, so we stumbled upon their car first. We were clueless to the fact that we had switched vehicles.

Even though my relationship with my parents had improved and we had funny adventures as a family, like the great car swap, I still hated going to high school. All these years later, I can see the dread that hung over my dead eyes in my senior picture.

When I graduated from high school, I hated being the center of attention so much that if I could have graduated from high school without crossing the stage, I would have. I won several academic and fitness awards, but at the ceremony I hoped and prayed that I would not hear my name called again. As I sat in my seat with my heart racing after accepting my diploma and awards, I decided that the next time that I was on stage, I would be there without fear. I would celebrate my achievement instead of fearing the recognition. I knew I would be graduating again in four years—I had a timeline to conquer my fear.

I chose Lewis & Clark College during Spring break of my senior year of high school. My mom had scoured college pamphlets looking for the right place to send me. My parents said I could go to any college I could get myself into. I set my sites on Oregon, Washington or Colorado in search of mountains, green scenery and getting as far away from Texas as possible. My parents sent me alone to investigate Willamette University, Evergreen University and Lewis & Clark College. These three good schools couldn't be any more different if they tried.

I arrived at Evergreen University in Olympia, Washington, only to find I was being housed overnight in a co-ed dorm. One of my roommates was actually getting a degree in rainbows. *Rainbows!* I called my parents from a pay phone and declared Evergreen was off the list.

Our longtime family friend Pat picked me up and I made my way down to Willamette University in Salem, Oregon. When we arrived, the campus was nearly vacant. I thought maybe I had arrived during their break, but it was just a rainy day and everyone was inside. There, I discovered everyone was either in a sorority or fraternity. Even the people not in one of these organizations were labeled. I hated labels and clubs so I crossed Willamette University off the list.

I then made my way to Lewis & Clark College. When I arrived it was raining, but the campus was buzzing with activity. People were out playing hacky sack, running with dogs and socializing everywhere on the beautiful campus. I was hooked. I called my parents and told them I was going to Lewis & Clark College.

My decision caused new concerns for my parents, because out of all the schools I had applied to, Lewis & Clark was the only college I hadn't been accepted to yet. I wasn't worried, but my mom fretted. She wanted me to make a "plan B," just in case. I sarcastically told her I'd stay in Texas with her. That caused her even more anxiety until she realized I was kidding, but I was still unwilling to make an alternate plan. I think my mom was the most excited in our family when my acceptance letter arrived.

Chapter 9
Portland, Oregon (1986–1992)

With college, the opportunity I craved to reinvent myself was upon me. I was intensely frightened of speaking in public. I decided I was going to show up on my first day of college and pretend this fear didn't exist. I arrived in my first class, and I had resolved to talk out loud in class and to participate whether I had anything to say or not.

As we sat around a round table discussing the book *To Know a Fly* by Vincent G. Dethier and N. Tinbergen, I opened my mouth repeatedly to speak and nothing came out. Finally, before class ended, I got my words out, even though my hands were shaking violently under the table. Over time, I forced myself through class after class speaking up while my hands shook, until one day, my hands stopped shaking and my voice grew confident. Eventually, I was truly no longer frightened of speaking in public.

During those four years, I became quite outspoken in the classroom, did many poetry readings, became a leader in student government and served on many committees. Somewhere along the way, I lost track of the girl with the fear of speaking. With time, my body forgot to shake violently.

I had been more than ready to go away to college, but I wasn't thrilled that I couldn't bring Puffy with me. When I graduated from high school, I literally walked out of the ceremony, posed for pictures and walked away from everything and everyone related to my two years of school in San Antonio. I never looked back. When I left for college, I thought I would never step foot in San Antonio again. I was counting on my parents being transferred overseas before my winter break. That fall, when I got the news the transfer wasn't going to happen in time, I was devastated.

I didn't want to go back to a place full of difficult memories. I had run away and mentally burned all bridges that led to San Antonio. I remember walking back to my dorm reading the letter from my parents totally crushed. I ran into my friend, Van, who was the happiest person on earth. I told him how desperately I never wanted to return to San Antonio, even if it was only for a six-week winter break.

I have never forgotten what Van said to cheer me up. It was a typical rainy, dreary, grey Northwest day.

"There is always a patch of blue sky no matter how bad things are," he said.

We scanned the grey skies, but I couldn't find a patch of blue.

He said excitedly, "Wait for it, and it will come. Even if you don't see it right now, it will appear."

Sure enough, as we stood there in the pouring rain, a tiny patch of blue sky appeared. It was small in the vastly dark sky, but it was there. He promised me that just like the patch of blue sky appeared, so would something good come from returning to San Antonio.

Facing My Fears

I went home that winter break, and it turned out I needed surgery, which I never would have been able to get done if we had been overseas during that break. I recovered in the safety of my parent's home and never had to venture out into my old world. Nothing bad happened and the memories didn't consume me. I discovered I could face my fears and return to hard times as a stronger and better person.

Puffy was thrilled to have me home. I don't know when it started; it just always was that way for as long as I can remember. Every night Puffy would go to bed with me with her paws wrapped around my neck and her head resting on one side of my neck. She spent the entire night with me flip flopping as necessary to follow me around the bed. It was such a habit. When I went away to college, my parents ended up buying me a teddy bear before they left taking pity on my inability to sleep with empty arms. I named him Teddy's Elmer's Glue, but I called him Elmer for short.

My dad had hidden his middle name from me for many years as a child. I never understood why. I coaxed, asked and begged. Eventually he relented and told me his middle name was Elmer.

I asked, "Like Elmer's Glue?"

My dad laughed until he snorted and replied, "Now that's one I have never heard."

And to me, my teddy bear filled the void of Puffy for a few years and served as a reminder that my family was the Elmer's Glue that held me together.

The "blue sky" my friend had promised me appeared when my parents were transferred to Germany just before my summer break after my freshman year. The timing of their transfer was perfect. We lived the entire summer in a hotel in Offenbach, Germany. We didn't have to spend our time moving into the new house, we got to live in a hotel with Puffy and Willie, and we were in a country we loved at exactly the right moment in our lives.

My dad was new at his post, so he wouldn't let my mom and I get jobs at the only place to work on base. He would have been our boss and he was strictly against nepotism. So without having to work, we were able to wander, have adventures and bond as never before. Because we were new in the city, my parents and I only had each other. We loved every moment there, being strangers together.

Had things happened according to my timing, my parents would have moved prior to my winter break, but my timing would have been all wrong. Many times in life, I have searched the dark clouds for a promised tiny patch of blue—and I always find it, literally and figuratively.

Lessons about Life in Autumn

After summer break, I returned to Lewis & Clark College for my sophomore year. That autumn, I found myself sitting on campus among my friends mourning the death of one of our own. Still today when the leaves change colors each year, I'm reminded of the outdoor celebration we held to honor my friend's life. Just a few days prior his memorial celebration, I had passed Troy in the cafeteria as I rushed out the door. I waved at him. The look on his face told me I should spend a few minutes with him. In fact, every fiber of my body told me to stop to talk to him. But I was in a hurry. I pushed aside my instinct and rushed out the door. I never saw him alive again.

He had leukemia. Because he still lived on campus, the reality of the disease never set in for me—until the word spread he had died.

I cried out into the void that his loss left in my life, "If only!"

This painful lesson reminds me we don't know the number of our days. It is easy to get caught up in the busyness of life and rush past a moment in which we should linger. Now it's my mission to stop and savor important moments. I always listen to my instinct to call people or pray for them when they suddenly come to mind.

I also try to never ignore a look saying "I need you to connect with me." I know there are days when my humanness shows and I fail at my daily mission. But, with each sunrise, I embrace my mission anew.

I remember almost everything about the moment that I rushed past Troy without stopping to talk. I can still hear the sounds around me and smell the aroma of the cafeteria. I clearly recall the look on his face as he was asking me to linger for a moment. I distinctly remember the feeling I had as I rushed away. The only thing I don't remember is what I was rushing to do.

Autumn always reminds me of the brevity of life. I still feel a lump in my throat in response to the opportunity I lost. Although now, crimson leaves also remind me to slow down and enjoy every golden moment of life.

Experiencing the Influence of A Mentor

Part of the reason I wanted to go to Lewis & Clark College was because of its international program. I set my sights on going on the Ireland trip my sophomore year and I went with twenty-four other students from Lewis & Clark College. It was an opportunity of a lifetime in so many ways. The trip was led by Dr. Helena Carlson, a professor of psychology, also from Lewis & Clark College.

As a young college student, I had no idea Helena would be the most influential teacher of my entire educational process. Helena was that monumentous in my life not because she was the leader of my trip, or a professor in the department I majored in, but because she taught me to think for myself. I always knew what Helena's opinion was on any topic, but she never wanted us to parrot her. She wanted us to research and decide where we stood on every topic. She challenged us to think independently.

Part of her method of teaching us about the history of Ireland was having speakers come from both the Protestant and the Catholic perspectives. We heard from political leaders on both sides of the aisle and both sides of the abortion controversy. No subject was taboo for Helena and we never got only one side of any argument—ever. She taught us to do research and make a decision only after collecting and evaluating all of the information. It was forbidden to only research the side of an argument you already believed to be right. All research had to be fair and balanced.

I found my balance under the wings of Helena. I learned to research, weigh opinions and decide for myself what I believed about every subject. I think I began to fully grow up and become Kayla in Ireland. There was nothing "Blue" about me anymore. I was me. I knew what I thought. I could speak up for myself. I felt empowered in a new and tangible way.

Helena transplanted us into the lives of people who were living out the subject that we were studying. We visited a Traveler's Camp (the local term for gypsy community), we went into Northern Ireland (don't tell anyone of authority at Lewis & Clark or our parents), we worked in internships, went to the theatre, hitchhiked around Ireland, had spontaneous adventures and so much more. We truly experienced Ireland, her people, her land, her controversy and her love story. And once we had studied and lived her story, we had opinions that were validated and worthy of holding firm to.

I still lean on what I learned from Helena. I honestly don't have an opinion on a subject until I have done my research. I don't believe anything strongly until I know I have looked at it from every angle. Once I have thoroughly researched a topic, I am willing to express my opinion. I tend to be a thinker and not a reactor because of this process I learned from Helena.

Forging Ahead Alone When Necessary

I learned one particular weekend in Ireland that sometimes, you have to forge ahead alone when you have a goal. My journey with friends to reach the Cliffs of Moher taught me this lesson. During our trip, students had to spend four days a week going to classes and the other three days we were free to travel the country.

On our trip to see the Cliffs of Moher, we hitchhiked from Dublin, and we ran into many obstacles along the way to the remote town of Doolin. Our original plan was to reach Doolin by late afternoon and walk up the Cliffs of Moher from there. But our journey took much longer than we expected.

The roads to Doolin were not heavily traveled. We walked for hours between seeing cars pass. We finally learned that if we went to the local post office, we could ride in the back of the mail truck out to Doolin. It was a painfully slow trip, because we had to stop many times along the way to deliver the mail.

Finally, as the sun was beginning to set, we arrived in Doolin. We knew it was a ten minute drive to the Cliffs, but we were on foot. My traveling partners were discouraged and exhausted, but I had set my mind on reaching the Cliffs. The wind was throwing its weight around and we knew a terrible storm was coming. Our only option out of town was on the mail truck first thing in the morning the next day. It was clear the only way to see the Cliffs we had traveled so far to see was to start running towards the ocean.

My friends decided that the journey had wiped them out and that they would skip seeing the Cliffs of Moher. I decided that I could not and would not give up on my quest to see them. I took off, running up the long hill and cutting across acres of land. As I ran through the fields, I leapt over rock walls and attracted the attention of a local dog. He ran up enthusiastically beside me.

As the dog and I ran, we also caught the attention of a lone sheep grazing in the field. Soon the dog, the sheep and I were racing towards the Cliffs of Moher, while a storm whipped the air around us. As I drew closer to the Cliffs, I could literally taste the ocean as the salt water blew hundreds of feet into the air and touched me. I stopped at the top of the Cliffs to admire the view. I was surrounded by the greenest green grass, which dramatically ended at the majestic cliffs. The cliffs dropped 700 feet into a raging, storming ocean. The sun was setting as I gazed upon the most satisfying, grandiose view of the rugged beauty of Ireland that I had ever had the privilege to see. The dog sat by my side while the sheep waited a few feet away. It was quite a sight to behold.

In that moment, I knew I was witnessing the raw beauty of an undisturbed vantage point that would resonate in my soul for a lifetime. In every direction I looked, there was no other human being. I was completely alone with the wonders of creation. I sat there embracing the experience and writing poetry, eternally grateful I did not give up on this moment.

As darkness set in, I walked back to town slowly, not wanting to leave the experience behind. I knew I would never be able to convey to my traveling companions what I had just witnessed. We had seen many glorious places, experienced unforgettable moments together, but nothing could ever compare to the experience I just had. I left the sheep in his field while the dog followed me back to town. We arrived wind-whipped, exhausted, and at the same time, incredibly energized.

Determined to Reach Our Destination

On another day of our journey, my two friends and I ventured out to see the Lakes of Killarney. The lake was so placid and beautiful. We were walking around the shores admiring the sheer beauty of the setting. We started talking about how we wished we had a boat to take out onto the crystal clear waters. Believe it or not, just then, we came upon a man standing along the shore with a boat. We asked him if we could borrow his boat to go out onto the water. The Irish are the most generous people I've ever met; he actually put the boat in the water and let us row away without him in the boat.

Sometimes, I think the memories I have from my time in Ireland must have been dreams because they seem so surreal. But this memory wasn't a dream. Off we went, rowing out into the middle of the lake in a borrowed boat. It was a perfect ideal day in the most beautiful place in the world. We were admiring the wonder of it all when suddenly a storm came in from out of nowhere. The smooth, calm water became choppy as the wind raged around us. The wind blew so hard that it seemed our attempts to get back to shore were useless. We rowed ten times harder to escape the storm than we had rowed to get out on the lake.

We met our challenge initially with laughter. We imagined the guy who owned the boat was safe and sound in his home totally unaware of the drastic turn our journey had taken. We hoped he wouldn't find his rowboat ship-wrecked or capsized. We determined we had no option but to keep rowing, laughing and rowing until eventually we reached our goal. Finally, we reached the shore, put the boat back where it belonged and headed back to our youth hostel. Just as we were about to escape the storm into the safety of the indoors, it stopped just as suddenly as it had started.

Life is full of storms—unexpected and unplanned. It is all in how you weather it. Life is all about the attitude embraced to face its storms. Sometimes we find ourselves rowing ten times as hard to get to the same place, and that is okay.

While I was studying in Ireland, I experienced many other traveling adventures around the country. Another one of my favorite memories is my journey with two friends to the town of Dingle. We thought we had left Dublin in plenty of time to hitchhike to Dingle with time to spare. Because we had spent many trouble-free months thumbing our way through Ireland, we did not anticipate the problems we encountered on the road down the Dingle Peninsula. Our struggles getting to the Cliffs of Moher paled in comparison.

We found ourselves walking for hours along the road that led to Dingle waiting for any car to pass. When a rare car drove down the road, we literally got on our knees and begged for them to stop and pick us up. But no one was going to Dingle because the majority of traffic to and from Dingle was via fishing boat. As we stood along the empty road, we discovered the value of choosing the right vehicle to get to your destination.

Hours into our journey, we were trying to come up with an alternative plan that would get us somewhere safe for the night. We were not willing to detour from our desire to see Dingle and no other plans worked to get us to our destination. So, we walked along the road turning back repeatedly to look for any sign of a car. Finally, past dinnertime and before sunset, a lone car pulled over and drove us into Dingle. The driver informed us no one hitchhikes to Dingle. We nodded in exhausted agreement.

When we arrived in Dingle, we were starving, but we headed directly to the youth hostel. We discovered that a youth group from France had filled the entire youth hostel. There was literally no room at the inn for us. We found ourselves at our goal destination, after dark, walking down the road, exhausted and dejected walking back towards downtown Dingle. We had nowhere to stay and no way back out of town. None of us had enough money to stay in a hotel, there was no bus out of Dingle. We had already proven there was no traffic along the Peninsula to hitchhike out.

We wandered into a local pub to eat and to figure out what to do next. The owner of the pub inquired about our long faces. We explained our situation. She took our food order and soon after returned to our table with more food than we had ordered. She told us we could stay in her home above the pub for the next two nights at no charge. We had all been away from home for a long time and the luxury of living in the pub owner's home for two nights was heaven sent.

My journey to Dingle was memorable for many reasons. I got to experience true hospitality first hand. I learned that there really are "roads less traveled" and they are worth adventuring down. But more than anything else, the experience gave me an image to refer to in my mind when I need to weigh whether I am riding in the right vehicle to my destination. Am I heading to a fishing village down a deserted road? Or, am I heading to a fishing village on a fishing boat? If I am on the deserted road, is the journey worth the heartache, and if so, am I traveling with friends?

Eventually our trip to Ireland ended. I spent the summer in Germany before heading back to Portland for my junior year of college. Puffy was always happy to have me home, but after I left, my parents reported she would mourn my departure with yowls that echoed through the house.

Overcoming Lingering Fears

I still had one fear to conquer in college. I set out to cure myself once and for all of my fear of water. During my junior year, I took sail boating to purposely do something I was uncomfortable with on the water. It turned out that I actually loved sailing. I had spent time out on boats, but nothing brings you as close to the water as sailing. I loved it when the cold water of the Willamette River would splash up onto my face.

In college, I was right at home in the party scene. I never just hung out with one group of friends; I had many different groups of friends. Not everyone was up to drinking every night of the week, but I was. I diversified with my friendships. Every night I always had at least one friend to drink with if not an entire party to participate in. I lived in a co-ed dorm. The floor I lived on was all girls, but the floors below us and above us were both occupied by boys. Lewis & Clark only had two fraternities and one was more organized than the other. The organized fraternity was housed on the floor below us. They nearly always had a party or a group of drinkers in the lounge.

Lewis & Clark also had sports I was unfamiliar with. They had a lacrosse and a rugby team. I was fascinated by both sports, but even more excited that both revolved heavily around booze. I went to one of the lacrosse games at played at Reed College with some of the older girls that I knew who drove. After the game, we went to a party with some of the lacrosse team and spectators. The party dwindled down to about six of us late into the night and ended up in my dorm room. Most of the people in our group were people I had never met other than one girl from my floor.

After much boozing, the party dwindled down and I found myself alone with a guy I had not met before that night. I tried to boot him out of my room so I could go to bed in the wee hours of the morning. I had no interest in getting to know him. He had other plans. He started kissing me and I, more adamantly, stopped him and stated it was time for him to go. He threw me down and pinned me on my bed.

He insisted, "I know you want me, I know you want me!"

To which I replied, "No. I don't want you. It is time for you to go."

I wrestled and fought until I realized there was no hope of me winning in a physical match against this much larger athletic man. For a moment, being eight years old in Desoto flashed through my mind and then San Antonio. A dust storm of old hurt kicked up inside of me. And in a forever second, I chose not to go dead inside this time. I refused to vanish into myself. My brain fought back. I stopped physically fighting. I was suddenly fully sober. I was well acquainted with trauma. I knew it well. I could smell my fear.

I said, "Okay, Okay, you are right. I do want you. But I have to go the bathroom first."

He was so full of himself that he believed me.

He gleefully said, "I knew it. Okay, hurry back."

He released me.

I walked calmly out of my room. As soon as the door shut behind me, I ran for help. My friend entered my room and escorted him out. They found him naked in my bed waiting for me.

Above all, I had escaped being raped. As I was in these compromising situations, I really didn't wonder how one person could be a victim so many times. It wasn't until much later that I realized that my drinking was putting me in the wrong place, in the wrong state of mind, at the wrong time and with the wrong people. I played a major role in creating the situations that made me wallow in self-hatred. These were not random events, but almost all centered around drunken parties where no one was thinking straight. I didn't ask for it, but had I not been drunk and alone with men who were willing to take what they wanted, I would not have been their victims.

During my senior year, I continued my quest of conquering my fear of water by taking a scuba diving elective. On day one my scuba instructor pulled me aside to ask if someone was forcing me to take this class since I had fear written all over my face. I informed him that I was forcing myself and shared my fears with him. He allowed me to do my early underwater training in the shallow end of the pool. He told my classmates I was having trouble with my ears.

It was a long hard road for me to go from the shallow end to the deep end to the murky deep cold waters of the Puget Sound, where our class traveled for our final exam. I had come too far to be willing to accept failure. My instructor warned me that he was going to be extra hard on me. It is dangerous to give into fear while scuba diving. He informed me that he needed to be assured that I would not panic deep under water and dart to the surface causing a dangerous air embolism—a condition that can cause a heart attack.

I was about to face drowning, one of my greatest fears, by becoming a certified scuba diver in the cold waters of the Puget Sound. We traveled in a college van to the Sunrise Motel for our weekend of certification testing. I had only previously conquered the deep end of the swimming pool in my scuba gear.

The waters of the Puget Sound where rough and had been churned up so much causing visibility to be minimal. Nothing was going to stop me from getting certified because it was a pass or fail college credit based on successful certification. I was in the last semester of my senior year and on the verge of accomplishing a 4.0 grade point average for the first time, and I had set a goal to conquer my fear before I graduated. My only option was to become a certified scuba diver and overcome my fears or fail at two goals at once.

The first day of diving was easy. It was designed to make us feel comfortable in the frigid temperatures while we explored the shallow waters close to shore. On the second day, the two planned dives stoked the flames of all my fears, chased down all my weak points and challenged me to choose not to quit no matter what. On my first dive of the second day, it was hard to say which was louder—my heart racing or my rapid breathing—as I dove into the cold darkness that engulfed me.

Under normal conditions, dive number one would have been a major stumbling block for me, but to make matters worse, visibility was so bad it was impossible to see my hand in front of my face. Our first dive was to forty feet with our diving buddy. Because the visibility was so awful, we had to follow a rope with our hands into pure darkness.

With each kick of my fins, the pressure increased and the temperature dropped further. It felt like a ring of ice pressed against my face in the only spot between my mask and wetsuit, where my skin touched the water unprotected. We dove blindly until we literally ran into our instructor at the bottom of the ocean floor. He put his mask up to each of our masks, one by one, so we could see eye-to-eye for a moment. Then, he vanished.

In the cold darkness I held onto the hand of my dive partner as we waited. This dive was designed to create crisis under water to put our training into action. Before I knew it, the sound of my breathing stopped as I sucked in for air and nothing was there. My instructor had come behind me and turned off my air. With absence of vision, I found my dive partners face, tapped on his respirator to signal I needed to buddy breathe. I forced myself to maintain calm as I attempted to communicate my need to share my partner's air. Every nerve in my body wanted to push upwards towards the surface of the water where the air was free and abundant. We successfully shared his respirator, and a few minutes later, my instructor turned my air back on. He came mask to mask with me. I could see that he was smiling with pride through his eye contact. I had overcome one of my greatest fears.

I tried to smile back. Just the thought of him potentially pulling off my mask at any moment filled me with the flee instinct. As he vanished out of view from me he pulled off my mask. At that very instant, everything in me wanted to quit the challenge. Clearing my mask underwater had proven to be my greatest obstacle of all. There was just something about all the water around my nose that made me throw all logic out and filled me with panic. It felt like an eternity in which I wrestled with irrational thoughts, panic and sheer fear coupled with an overwhelming desire to succeed. Finally, I put the mask back on my face, felt the water trapped inside the mask against my nose and, with all my will, I forcibly blew air via my nose to clear my mask.

I knew I was home free as my instructor's gleaming eyes peered into my mask once again. The rest of the tasks were mundane and he moved on to challenge my diving partner. I sat in the dark, holding hands with my unseen partner and waited. My heart danced, my breathing calmed and I celebrated. I had one last dive to do, but I knew despite the greater depth of the dive, I had done everything that I needed to accomplish my goal. The deep dive had to be taken with the instructor instead of our dive buddies because of the poor visibility. During that dive, I sat at the bottom of the ocean with eighty feet of water over head and realized no matter the weight of my challenge, the depth of my fear, or the close proximity of perceived danger, I had it in me to overcome anything.

I discovered that I could never let fear hold me back from anything. I gained an absolute impatience with fear that forces me to fight back against it. Do not allow a fear of failing to keep you from starting. You can only fail if you don't try. Even if it takes years to succeed and you fall down many times along the way, you have not failed as long as you get back up and keep going.

We all have fears and we all have the ability to overcome them. The difference between those who overcome their fears and those who don't is the direction in which the overcomers are walking. Those who overcome their fears walk towards them eye-to-eye, face-to-face. They challenge the validity of their fears. Those who do not overcome fears walk away from what they are fearful of, surrendering before triumph is claimed, giving up on the dream of a victory dance. Come dance—despite fear—and run toward the challenge, because all goals lie on the other side of your own personal set of obstacles.

Puffy Returns

During my senior year of college, Puffy came to live with me. I was blessed with the opportunity to spend three months of summer and six weeks of winter in Germany every year. But I missed being on the same continent with Puffy. She was twenty years old and traveled in a small carrier under my seat on the airplane. I was ecstatic to have Puffy moving into my new life with me. During my senior year in college—just like she had been in grade school—Puffy became a fixture on campus.

By this time Puffy moved slow, steady and confident. I carried a small bed with me that I put next to my chair during class. She would meander into class behind me, crawl into her bed and nap through class. Once class was out, I woke her up and she would follow me back to my car. She preferred to think of herself as my equal and a partner who walked beside me. Puffy was not a pet. In our lives together, she was my loyal friend. As far as she was concerned, when she was with me, she was home, and home was mobile.

Puffy had had a notoriously bad bladder her entire life, but in the final years, it was even worse. I learned to fly across the room to move her quickly to her cat box at the slightest hint of an accident. She started to think any crinkly sound below her feet signified she had reached her cat box. If I heard her tiny feet hit paper, plastic bags or any other material which provided a sound effect, I moved in quickly to swoop her to the nearest litter box. She wasn't malicious about her peeing, simply confused. I never punished her—what was the point at twenty years old.

Her life became about sitting on my lap, following me around, going to bed with me and finding a place to relieve herself based on sound effects. During her twentieth winter, it snowed in Portland. After countless memories of traipsing through the snow with Puffy, I was excited to take her out to adventure with me. Her age was made abundantly apparent as she winced when her feet touched the cold snow. She found no interest in anything about the snow other than finding a path out if it. Our childhood was officially over.

During that winter, my boyfriend's granddad was dying. I loved Cecil as if he was my own family. He had fallen broken his hip. We had to put him in a rehabilitation center. There we discovered he had cancer too. We visited often. The nurses would turn their eyes and shake their heads as we burst through the doorway disturbing the deadly silence which slumbered within. Cecil begged us to break him out. We would try to give him a piece of freedom by taking him for wheelchair rides in the parking lot. On one occasion, we left three sets of footprints and one pair of wheelchair tracks engraved in the snow of the otherwise empty parking lot.

Cecil told us stories about his childhood as he mumbled about the cold, covered in a sweater, jacket, blanket, hat and umbrella. His wheelchair had gathered wet sticky snow within its spokes, and it dropped melting clumps of slush onto the clean and shiny floor of the convalescent home. We left the trail of pleasure only to return him to grumpy nurses who had let him get bed sores.

We laughed down the hallways, passing immobile wheelchairs and bedridden faces on our way back to his room. We removed his wet layers, returning him to slippers and his favorite chair. We had forgotten what he was doing there, until we watched him pant in exhaustion through his thin shirt, and his fading size was again made apparent.

For a moment we had seen him young again. He was the man in the green hat, carrying a red and blue umbrella, covered in a lime green blanket, dancing in the snow with us. When spring came, we carried Cecil out of the convalescent home against the doctor's wishes. He was dying and he wanted to die at home. I often brought Puffy over to sit with him. They would sit in the chair together for hours. He would shift and she would reposition. They both had old bones. They would doze off together. As we tended to Cecil's needs, Puffy tended to his heart. In March I picked the first flowers of spring, and Cecil died. His loss was hard to face.

I spent my senior year busy with classes. A local department store had hired me part-time as a supervisor on one side of town. On the other side of town, I worked an internship a local high school in the counseling department.

I was twenty-three years old and Puffy was on the verge of her twenty-first birthday. And snow had become only a matter of discomfort. Other than her slow gate, her greying fur and accident-prone condition, I had been able to ignore her aging state. I convinced myself that Puffy and I would live on as a team for many years. I had lost count of how she had used up her nine lives.

The winter snow melted into spring and my college graduation was quickly approaching. Puffy's Siamese brown markings began to show through her solid black fur. Puffy had a cracked front tooth and horrendously bad breath. I started making plans for Puffy to celebrate her twenty-first birthday at the Fulton Pub. People brought their dogs there and they were not even twenty-one years old! *So why not bring my cat?* I submitted Puffy's birthday to Willard the Weatherman on the *Today Show*. I figured he announced birthdays of people who turned one hundred years old, so it was worth asking him to announce a cat turning one hundred and forty seven in cat years. It was a long shot, but through the years I had learned that there was no harm in asking.

A few days before her birthday, Puffy woke up in obvious pain. She had never been sickly. Yes, she had made many visits to the vet for emergencies, but not because of being sick. I had heard of some cats that lived into the thirties. I just assumed Puffy would be one of those cats. I had never prepared myself for her to get sick. I figured she had a long life ahead of her since she was no longer in danger of getting hit by a car, eating a lizard whole, getting stung by a scorpion or other bizarre events. I rushed Puffy to the vet thinking surely she had eaten something that was making her feel ill.

I was completely and utterly shocked when the vet told me Puffy's kidneys were shutting down. I had the choice to take her home and keep her comfortable for as long as possible or to let the vet put her down right then and there. My mind was numb with shock. She hadn't been sick just the day before; suddenly, she was at death's door.

I chose to take her home and keep vigil over her for as long as she was comfortable. I simply was ill-prepared to say goodbye. My job and schoolwork ceased to matter. I took Puffy home to begin to say goodbye. My parents were living in a different time zone and this decision felt like the first adult decision that I had to face alone.

Puffy had officially used up all of her nine lives and I needed to walk with her through our final goodbye.

I sat on the balcony of my home rocking, soothing and petting Puffy. As time passed that night, it turned out to be Puffy who did more comforting to me than I was doing for her. She purred for hours and licked away my constant stream of tears. Her pain began to increase in the middle of the night. I deeply regretted the selfish decision I had made to bring her home. Puffy began to yowl in pain in between her purring. We spent the night and early morning hours sitting together, each trying to comfort the other.

When morning came, I placed Puffy in her bed on the passenger seat of my car. We drove across Portland to my vet. I sobbed the entire way. I didn't even have to open my mouth when I arrived at the vet with red swollen eyes. I held Puffy cradled in her bed so I wouldn't disturb or move her in any way could cause more pain. I set her warm bed on the cold stainless steel counter and waited for the vet.

I could barely get the words out. Yes, put her to sleep. Yes, I want to be here when you give her the drugs to relax her. No, I can't be here for the second shot which takes her life. And so I left her still breathing, but unconscious as I stumbled out into the waiting room leaving behind my best friend, the one I had never faced a day without her. I was inconsolable as I wrote a check to pay. I'm sure the woman at the counter wished she could simply wave me on without payment as an uncomfortable hush rushed over the other pet owners in the waiting room.

I tried to move on with the plans I had earlier made for the day to go out on the Willamette River waterskiing. I tried. I went. But I simply sat on the back of the boat looking out onto the wake left by our boat sobbing about the life behind me. I had never lived a full day I remembered without Puffy breathing in my home or my parent's home. Distance sometimes separated us, but she was always there—ever present—interwoven into my history as my best friend and companion.

I couldn't get past the memory of her dying in my arms with her only concern being me. She purred and licked away my tears as her body gave out on her. She was a scrappy little cat, who throughout the years taught me and re-taught me the lesson of perseverance. I knew I had to move on. I knew logically that Puffy was just a cat. But she had been my cat. She had been my best friend. Her life hemmed in the corners around my childhood. Without her, I was no longer a child. She had been the cornerstone of my memories. Always present, always there at the end of any day to be with me, love on me, purr for me and comfort me. Now, when I needed her comfort the most, she was gone. Gone forever.

Chapter 10
After Puffy (1992)

After Puffy died, graduation was around the corner. Activity was everywhere and I was simply sad. I now had the dead pet to write sad poetry about. I was in a bad place in my life even before her death and didn't even know it. I was in a bad relationship, and all of my plans were intertwined with his. I was engaged to a man who was mentally abusive and controlling. I didn't have any plans to move on in a healthy direction. I stayed in my rut and mourned.

Mother's Day wasn't far behind Puffy's death. I remember calling my mom to tell her that I loved her and to have a happy day. But she could hear that I was terribly sad and literally falling apart inside. She asked me about my plans, and I told her I had none; I said I couldn't make any because I had left my body so that I wouldn't cry in public places.

Right there as I answered her, my emotions crashed down on me, leaving me speechless as I gulped for air and found I had none. My poor mom tried to stretch her arms through the phone lines. She listened to my voice break as I cried alone on a public phone in a mall filled with strangers. I stared at the freight elevator and dreamed it could take me far enough to reach my mom, help me pass through the thousands of miles that separated us, so that she could actually hold me.

I cried into the tiny holes of the public telephone, splashing my mom's face with the sorrow of a child she could not hold. She nearly cried too when I told her that after Puffy died, even the house kitten had died. *But what could she do?* The buzz of the phone grew louder as we called out to each other, "I love you." And then there was silence. And I was left standing alone, crying in a mall of strangers.

The next month my parents came to America for my graduation from college. I was living like a manic depressive—happy one moment until the next wave hit when I became dark and remorseful. We were celebrating my graduation from college and my recent engagement. I graduated with honors. I had managed to get a 4.0 and landed on the Dean's list during my final semester of college. I think I reached my full potential as a student that semester only because the students I counseled in the drug and alcohol program had challenged me to stop drinking with them. I never confessed to having a problem, but they figured if they couldn't drink, then I should take the challenge with them. I took them up on it and found school was a whole lot easier sober.

It was a rainy wet day in Portland, Oregon, when I graduated. I remember my brother popping a champagne bottle as we stood under a tree posing for pictures.

I wondered, "What harm can a glass of champagne do?"

I partook in the celebration toasting with champagne. And with that, my first bout of sobriety ended. I spiraled back into drinking. I took my eyes off the problems of my engagement and kept moving forward in a sick relationship. And my heart still ached for Puffy.

One day, we got a call asking if I'd be willing to take in a Himalayan kitten someone had bought and later realized they were allergic to cats. My dream cat never included a Himalayan, but I fell in love with her beautiful non-snub nosed face. I named her Ena, because she was "a little ardent one" full of feisty character. I decided to leash train her so I could take my cat anywhere I went.

Ena was glad to play along because she was madly in love with me too. She was happy to sit on my shoulder and go anywhere with me. I took her to the beach, on the bus, through downtown Portland and even on a ferryboat. She didn't care where we went as long as we went together. I loved her, but she was no replacement for Puffy. My fiancé saw her as a means to control me further, threatening to keep her if I ever left him.

After graduation, I rose morning after morning, convincing myself that I had found happiness. I accepted where I was as where I should be day after day, waiting for the first lick of his voice to slap at my ears. It never failed every day he spoke, and I listened, believing as he did that he was always right, and I was always wrong.

"What is there to life when I am always wrong?" I began to ponder.

Days passed, and his voice ate at my soul. I heard in my head a scream for escape. Night after night, I went to sleep full of hate. Days were brittle and nights were stone cold.

I could hear in my head, "I hate you, I hate you…"

And then suddenly, the voice was aimed at him and not me. One day I rose within myself and left him wondering what had hit as I packed my life, Ena and all, and left, finally moving in the right direction. Once the motion began away from him, there was no stopping the momentum of my run.

Ena and I moved out with three hundred dollars in the bank. I borrowed a car for the weekend. I had gathered up just enough strength to stop the cycle of being a victim. I made a conscious decision to live my life as a survivor. I got hired almost immediately at Meier & Frank Department store in downtown Portland. I convinced a landlord I was good for the first and last month's rent even though I had nothing to put down on an apartment. I was ready to face anything.

Little did I know what "anything" could possibly mean for me. I was now a grown up and completely on my own for the first time. My life had been stained with badge of victimhood and I still wore it daily. I had taken to heart the messages of those who filled my mind with confusing and disorienting messages.

For as early as I can remember, I was always seeking God. A veil of darkness blurred my vision. I grew further from God despite an echo of His voice making me desire to seek Him. The years of putting myself in dangerous positions, fueled by mind-altering and inhibition-numbing drunkenness had caught up to me. I felt paralyzed by guilt and shame.

I was also feeling terrorized. My departure from my fiancé had not gone smoothly. I was unable to accept that I was moving on without him and that he needed to move on without me. Many nights I would come home to find him sitting on my doorstep waiting. He called both my home and work constantly. I left all his messages unanswered. I had said everything I needed to say at goodbye. I told him he was frightening me, and yet he couldn't hear me. I'd come home to find a rose inside my apartment from him. I'd look up at work and find him in the crowd staring in at me.

Some days I would listen to him. Remind him I was done. I was no longer willing to allow him to twist my words. I was no longer willing to be wrong about everything. I was moving in the right direction, away from him, but I couldn't get him to let go. I partied even harder to cope with my fear. I rebelled against his attempt to control me.

The party train abruptly ended. One morning, with no memory of the night before, I awoke feeling life inside of me. The feeling of life was foreign and altogether consuming as I had been so dead and so numb for so very long. I knew with certainty I was pregnant. Just as suddenly, I also knew life began at conception and I had to protect this new life with all of my being.

I was only hours pregnant when I chose to stop drinking for the good of my child. I had studied fetal alcohol syndrome in college, and, all these years later, I still haven't taken a single drink. I couldn't bear to injure this baby. I was instantly converted from being pro-choice to being ready to sacrifice everything to protect life, especially this life. My future plans to obtain my Ph.D. were quickly abandoned. They now become meaningless in the face of this new life.

I went to the store a week later to buy a pregnancy test and bottle of wine. I decided one or the other would be my future. The test came up positive, so I gave the bottle of wine to my neighbors.

The next day I went to confirm the test at a women's clinic. I stood beside the nurse waiting for the test results. It came up negative.

I insisted I was indeed pregnant. She administered another more accurate test. This one came up with a very faint positive sign.

The nurse turned to me and said, "Don't worry. It is early enough we can get this taken care of before you even know you're pregnant."

I suddenly realized the women's clinic I had gone to for help was, in reality an abortion clinic. I flew out of there never looking back.

Later that day in downtown Portland, I told the biological dad that I was pregnant. He and I had been friends since childhood.

I felt safe as I told him, "I am pregnant."

He turned to me and said, "Don't worry, I will be there," after a long pause, "for the abortion."

I replied, "I am not having an abortion."

"I didn't sign up to be a dad," he replied.

For the first time, I realized I had been playing Russian roulette with my life by making choices, that caused the creation of children. My resolve to protect my child grew. I settled in for a battle as pressure to abort my child continued to come from every direction.

Those around pressured me daily with arguments like, "Having this baby will ruin your life," and, "It would be better to have an abortion than to live with this mistake forever. At the very least, consider adoption and get on with your life."

I knew having this baby would save my life. I didn't know how, but I knew this child was a life preserver. I knew for me, adoption wasn't the best option. I was willing and able to let go of the future I had planned to grasp hold of the hope of a new future. I never wrestled with the decision to abort my baby because I knew I would never recover from it. I did take the time to wrestle with the decision of adoption.

Someone close to me said, "But you don't even like children."

To this I answered, "But I love this one."

With my love for my child solidified in my heart everything changed. I had thought my love for Puffy was as big as love got. I loved Ena, but her life had not yet weaved through the fabric of my life. I discovered a love bigger than I ever imagined possible as I faced pregnancy alone.

My parents were devastated by the news of my pregnancy. The hardest phone call I ever had to make was the international call to tell them. I sat on my futon listening to the unique sound of an international ring and gathered up my courage.

My mom answered, "Well, hello Kayla," in her familiar sing song voice.

I had to break her joy of hearing from me with difficult news.

My mom informed me, "You can't come home."

I replied, "I know."

I knew because my parents had been preparing me my whole life to live independently, to live with the consequences of my choices and to stand on my own two feet. There was no resentment between us as she let me know that door was closed. My brother was willing to do anything to help raise my baby. He always was my great protector.

As the months ticked by, I realized everything about my life was wrong. My belly grew and I searched in earnest for God. I visited church after church and denomination after denomination. I wanted to either prove the Bible as true or the whole Bible as false. In my mind, there could no longer be any half-truths. I used the critical thinking tools Helena had equipped me with and dug into the beliefs of multiple religions.

I wanted my child to have routine, roots and faith. I couldn't give it to him if I didn't find it on my own. I decided Jesus either was "The Way, the Truth and the Light," or He wasn't. Growing up, priests taught me the Bible was full of myths God used to teach us lessons. This spun me further into confusion.

As I entered my twelfth week of pregnancy, I started getting terrible abdominal pain. I was working at the time as a manager of a high fashion men's store. The owners of the store had come for a surprise inspection. They were angry to find out that I was pregnant. I thought the pain was because of the stress of their visit and continued working. But eventually the pain became too much to stand. I told them I was going home. They threatened to fire me if I did.

I turned to them as said, "I dare you to fire me for being pregnant."

I took the bus home and crawled into bed. The pain was overwhelming. I called my doctor's office for advice. The nurse informed me I was probably having a miscarriage. I asked to come in.

"Oh, honey nature will take its course. Sometimes there is something wrong with the baby and your body expels it," the nurse answered.

I wasn't okay with that answer. I called a nearby midwife office. She told me to come in. I didn't have a car so I called a friend. Through sobs, I asked her leave work and come get me. She did. We arrived at the midwife's office and she gave me cramp bark to take. She examined me. She soothed me and monitored my cramping. When the pain stopped she listened for my baby's heartbeat. I couldn't breathe until suddenly we heard the fast heartbeat of my baby.

I realized that I was in love with my baby. I was surprised that I was so terrified to lose my baby, one I never planned for, never expected and didn't know that I wanted. But I did want him and I did love him.

I continued to spend my pregnancy visiting the church services of every denomination I could find. As I nurtured the baby growing in my belly, I sought God. I tried to make a semi-committed relationship with the biological dad work out somehow. I packed up my life and moved temporarily to Seattle to give him an opportunity to fall in love with our son as I had.

The hardest decision I made was to give Ena away. I had found a job as an apartment manager to give me the freedom to work from home as soon as my son was born. Ena could not follow me to my new home. I was devastated as I said goodbye. Her new family offered to allow her to stay with me as I sobbed through my farewell with Ena. Saying goodbye to her seemed like the biggest of the sacrifices I was making, probably because it had the most instant results. The future I was giving up still seemed distant.

During my pregnancy, I cried more tears than I knew my body could produce. I was terrified. I was ill-equipped for motherhood and I knew it. I worked two jobs to save up extra money. My job as an apartment manager was physical as I painted and cleaned vacant apartments, fixed garbage disposals and various other odd jobs.

My second job was as teaching ESL (English as a Second Language) to Japanese students. My task was to walk with the student assigned to me throughout downtown Seattle and talk to them. The hills killed me as my belly grew.

Both of my employers were furious when they realized I was pregnant. They felt I should have disclosed it in our interviews, and maybe I should have, but I didn't allow being pregnant to stop me from any work that needed to be done. My ESL job was scheduled to end just a week before my due date. And I planned to only miss the day of my delivery at my apartment manager job.

A month before my due date, my son's biological dad let me know with all certainty his support would only be financial. He didn't want a relationship with me and didn't want to change his life to be a dad. I had wanted so badly to give my son everything, but I discovered I could only give him myself. The reality left me feeling bruised from the impact. I was faced with not only carrying half his life alone, but also parenting alone. I resolved to not be bitter in order to not fill my son's life with the sour grapes of anger and disappointment.

The week prior to my due date my mom arrived. My dad was scheduled to come after my son was born. She embraced me and my new life, even though she was terrified for me. She stood beside me as I delivered my son. She comforted me as I realized the pain of childbirth was beyond what I had ever imagined.

When they set my son on my stomach I wept. And for the first time in nine months, they were tears of joy. I was swept with an overwhelming love beyond anything I could have ever imagined. I had thought I knew what love was, but I was wrong. I only knew the outside edges of love. My love for my son, Keegan, was bigger than anything I could have ever dreamed.

I felt like I was born the day my son was born. I felt as if I was born with him. A whole new life opened up to me with new emotions. Motherhood expanded my heart. It opened me up to feel everything. All the parts of me that I had closed swung open in the first moments of motherhood. I knew my son was a life preserver thrown to me by someone bigger than I could imagine. When my dad arrived, I placed his first grandson into his arms. My dad wept. The strain between us blended into our overwhelming love for each other and my son.

After my parents returned to Germany, I dug deeper into my search for God. All my running, all my blaming and all my confusion ended when, several months after Keegan was born, I heard the "Good News" of Jesus Christ. I was a single mom, and instead of leaving me to suffer the consequences of my life, God tenderly rescued from the wilderness. He restored my broken life.

When the burdens of being responsible to answer to God for my actions alone were lifted from me, I was suddenly stronger than ever. I was fortified by the promises of God. Education, partying, people and travel never quenched my thirst for a purpose bigger than me. All the garbage of my past was redeemed; the shame forever cast as far as the East is from the West.

Motherhood and my new relationship with God defined me. I was content. I shredded up the victim sign I had worn for years and boldly faced the future. I was radically delivered from my previous addiction to alcohol. The sorrows of the past melted into the joy of motherhood. I learned my own language of motherhood. I had listened to the voice of my mom and extracted from her words a version of my own motherhood, separate and different than hers, however familiar. I claimed my own language. I wove my motherhood from my past, the present and our future.

As I looked over the sum of my life, I realized that I have stood by loved ones in their valleys and they've stood by in mine. I have been given the honor of being present at both the first and at the last breath of life. I have been the strong one stroking the belly of a loved one filled with cancer so advanced I could feel it under his thin skin. I was sitting beside him when his last breath escaped his body, relieved that his pain was over and mine had begun.

I have been the weak one weeping openly with bad news. I have been the adult, who felt like the little child trying to be brave, as Puffy passed away. My shoulders heaved as my legs barely held me as I wailed against the loss.

I have experienced the joy of celebration and hope and just as suddenly collapsed in despair. I wept into the tiny holes of the phone to my mom when loss was so common and constant, even my kitten died. I walked away from a future that would have destroyed me. I said goodbye when my heart wanted to stay. I ran away when warning bells rang.

I was guilty of causing heartbreak I couldn't undo. And I forgave those who would never ask for forgiveness. I had looked back over my life and surrendered my sins to Christ. And I was walking forward knowing that I had already been forgiven. I have lived through the complete spectrum of life—from ecstatic joy to dark grief—and learned valuable lessons along the journey.

I walked forward boldly, shoulders back, head held high as a survivor, a child of God and as the mother of my beloved son.

Acknowledgments

When I was young, I simply did not realize how lucky I was. My childhood home was mobile, but my family was stable. My dad taught me honesty, fearlessness and adventure while pouring out immeasurable love into my life. My mom gave me creativity, laughter and spunk through an unexplainable connection. My brother was my protector, closest ally and mischief maker while showing unflappable loyalty. And always in the mix of our family life were our beloved pets. My mom used to say, "You can pick your friends, but you can't pick your family." I thank God that He picked the perfect family for me.

Many thanks are owed to my editor Loral Robben Pepoon. She picked up this project and carried it home for me. Thanks to David Sanford for the role he played in making this book happen. David offered to read anything I wrote, but asked that I never send him a book about a cat. I followed all of his advice except this one point. I hope I prove him wrong about cat books. The input from my editing and critique team was priceless. Thank you Debbie Richards, Robin Schmidt, Rose Cunfer and Nora Kilbourne.

My cats Gogo and Star kept me company throughout the writing of this book. I am so thankful for the daily joy my cats share with me through their antics, quirks and drooling purrs.

I am inspired daily by my husband Dennis and my three children Keegan, Selah and Caiden. Most importantly, I praise my Lord Jesus for the gift of poetry, literature, animals and for the certainty of His saving grace. He redeemed my brokenness and freed me from the shame that consumed me for years. Through it all, He paired me with cats that nourished my heart and shared life adventures with me.

"And God made the beasts of the earth according to their kinds and the livestock according to their kinds, and everything that creeps on the ground according to its kind. And God saw that it was good." Genesis 1:25 ESV

About the Author

Kayla Fioravanti is living proof that the mind of a scientist can live concurrently with the heart of a poet in one body. Kayla's first three books published in 2011 include: *The Art, Science and Business of Aromatherapy, Your Guide for Personal Aromatherapy and Entrepreneurship; How to Make Melt & Pour Soap Base from Scratch, A Beginner's Guild to Melt & Pour Soap Base Manufacturing; and DIY Kitchen Chemistry, Simple Homemade Bath & Body Projects.* These books are all filled with scientific information spoken in plain English for the everyday reader. In 2012 Kayla published her first poetry book, *When I was Young I Flew the Sun Like a Kite*. In 2013 she published, *How to Self-Publish, The Author-preneur's Guide to Publishing*. In 2014 she was the managing editor and co-author of *360 Degrees of Grief, Reflections of Hope.*

Kayla and her family currently live in Franklin, Tennessee. She has been married to her husband Dennis since 1998 and has three children including Keegan, Selah and Caiden. You can follow Kayla at KaylaFioravanti.com.

About The Photographer

Shoot Y'all Photography was born out of a love for photography, cabin fever due to a snow storm, and the need to carve out a new journey. It's a strange combination, and one that flowed together like the words to a poem.

Lisa Rodger is a natural light photographer, she lives in the south, and she uses the word y'all…..a lot! Lisa loves candid, not posed. Flowing, not stiff. She shoots pictures based on the life that surrounds her clients. In addition to people, she shoots animals, landscape, architect, products and more. In a nutshell….she captures life!

Spending time with family and friends is what Lisa loves the most. In her spare time, you will likely find her on their sand volleyball court or simply relaxing in the country surrounded by twenty two fuzzy paper weights {aka cats}, and the love of her life, her husband Prevo.

www.ingramcontent.com/pod-product-compliance
Lightning Source LLC
Chambersburg PA
CBHW061325040426
42444CB00011B/2784